SCENES

The City

&

Society

a series of books edited by **GERALD D. SUTTLES**
University of Chicago

SCENES

by John Irwin

A SageMark Edition

 SAGE Publications / Beverly Hills / London

For information address:

SAGE PUBLICATIONS, INC.
275 South Beverly Drive
Beverly Hills, California 90212

SAGE PUBLICATIONS LTD
St George's House / 44 Hatton Garden
London EC1N 8ER

Printed in the United States of America

Library of Congress Cataloging in Publication Data

Irwin, John, 1929–
    Scenes

    (The City and society ; v. 1)
    Includes bibliographical references.
    1. Social interaction. 2. Sociology, Urban.
3. Social role. 4. City and town life—United
States. I. Title. II. Series.
HM131.I64   301.1   77-528
ISBN 0-8039-0823-7
ISBN 0-8039-0824-5 pbk.

FIRST PRINTING

Contents

To Marsha

Acknowledgements

My indebtedness starts with John Lofland, who encouraged me to undertake this book and then helped me at most stages until its completion. David Greenberg discussed most of the ideas with me, read drafts, and made many suggestions. Many people read chapters or the whole book and made valuable contributions, among them Herbert Blumer, Sherri Cavan, David Chandler, Gail Goldman, Stanford Lyman, Robert Perinbanayagam, and Marvin Scott. (I hope I haven't forgotten anyone.) Lyn Lofland and Gerald Suttles read it more than once and made heavy contributions. Billy Ray Bragg not only helped me greatly on an earlier study of surfing, which was used for this book, but read over the chapters on surfing and corrected historical mistakes. Charles Perry did the same for the history of hippies. To the extent this book reads well, Rhoda Blecker, of Sage Publications, gets the credit. Marsha Rosenbaum, my wife, read and listened to the book at least ten times and helped it and me.

J.I.

SCENES

Foreword

From the beginning of the Civil Rights Movement to Watergate marks off a period of intense self-examination for Americans. Historians may correct us by subsequent scholarship, but for those who came to maturity during this decade and a half, it seems set off as a definite period, with a beginning, middle, and end—certainly a watershed of some sort, although poorly charted and poorly understood. Now that the clouds have cleared a bit, we can begin to use some distance and detachment to gain a stronger grasp of the period's significance. This is not to say that there ever was any scarcity of intelligent commentary and analysis during the period, but sociology is an ongoing enterprise and aims at self-correction as well as at timeliness and relevance. This book by John Irwin asks us to reflect back and examine this period as observers rather than as participants.

The task is not an easy one, for memories are still fresh, and they continue to shape the undercurrents of relations between black and white, between young and old, between teacher and student, and between police and citizen. This period still provides us with much of our vocabulary for political debate, and the symbols of group membership which were achieved in this recent past are still frequently used to assess blame and take credit.

Like many of the rest of us, Irwin's interest in these social movements derives from his own experience; however, he has strenuously examined the evidence and the problems of evaluation and interpretation. Thus, this is both an intensely personal document and one that aims at the canons of detached interpretation. There can be no doubt that Irwin was in the thick of it during these troubled times. Yet, his effort is not to romanticize the recent past but to extract from these social movements their more durable consequences for urban life.

The result is an account which recognizes the rich development of emancipating ideas and at the same time the incapacity for group self-regulation among those sponsoring these ideas. Thus, efforts to create a freer and more voluntaristic way of life frequently went aground because of an inability to impose those ideas on a widening membership. Irwin traces this pattern with great care in the case of the hippies and surfers, and concludes that a group stressing a highly

11

voluntaristic style of life cannot survive an unselective effort at recruitment. Extreme forms of voluntarism, then, seem to be inherently unstable when these beliefs in voluntarism extend to the conditions of membership itself. Thus, the moral claims made by both hippies and surfers have been largely replaced by a sort of mass hedonism in which earlier vows of self-imposed poverty and ascetic athleticism have been displaced by custom-made jeans and mass-produced surfboards. Small pockets of genuine devotees remain, but they manage to survive largely by self-imposed isolation, and a low profile has replaced a previous, undifferentiated invitation to any and all.

As Irwin points out, both the hippies and the surfers had something more in mind than sheer mass hedonism. Both sought a more voluntaristic and less stratified society—a sort of celebration of life, and especially its expressive elements, irrespective of one's social background or social rank. Both movements included a positive endorsement of sensuality, of self-expression, and of candor. To a large extent, then, Irwin sees the hippies and surfers as attempting to extend to the masses a kind of play or expressive world that has regularly been the possession of some segments of the upper classes. The frank acceptance of premarital relations, the equal treatment of women, and the open discussion of taboo topics all have been previously included in some segments of cosmopolitan society. To the alarm of many, hippies and surfers alike sought to extend these freedoms to the majority of people—who, it was feared, could not be trusted with so much liberty.

In Irwin's view, however, neither the hippies nor the surfers could outlast the persistent problems that beset them, but this was less because of an individual inability to handle new-won freedoms than an inability to survive their inundation by opportunistic hangers-on. At their high point, both hippies and surfers possessed a relatively articulate "philosophy"—collectivist in the first, individualistic in the second. For those who moved gradually into each movement, this philosophy provided a regulative framework which was able to insure a considerable degree of reciprocity, mutuality, and contained self-expression. Socialization, however, was their only effective form of social control. As each movement achieved national prominence and as recruits multiplied, both the hippies and the surfers were transformed into an activity without an ideology. It is not that each became mere motion without meaning, but instead that each relapsed back into a well-worn mold in which competition, status-striving, conspicuous consumption, and domination by "star performers" were the most salient patterns. Some of the more idealistic adherents survive in self-imposed isolation, but it is

Irwin's observation that the most visible remnants represent little more than a corrupt and commercialized version of the "grand scene" of the 1960s. In less than one generation, it has passed from genuine to spurious culture.

This book, however, is not simply an obituary of a historic period and two of its social movements. Irwin is insistent—and I think that he is correct—that something more has been achieved and left as a heritage for successive generations. If current surfers and hippies are largely indistinguishable from other special consumer groups, the questions raised by their predecessors continue to circulate in more conventional circles. The status of women, the treatment of homosexuals, the legal rights of minors, the uses of pornography, the language we can voice in public, all of these are questions that continue to preoccupy us, and one does not have to have long hair or a bad school record to raise them. One does not even have to be under thirty years of age. What is most important, perhaps, is that these issues now preoccupy an enlarged public and have reached out to include submerged groups previously excluded from these arguments. We have moved a step closer to mass society, a society in which consensus and articulate debate are progressively more essential to its social order. It is not that coercion and authority have been altogether removed, but that a more diverse public has a larger voice in a range of issues that run from political choice to the morality of everyday life.

It is especially this sense of increased participation and self-awareness that Irwin points to as the chief residue of these social movements. The promptness with which different groups state their interests and their consciousness of the theatrical character of public life attest to new levels of emancipation and the voluntaristic basis for social order. Irwin is very much the optimist in seeing this as the beginning of a more articulate debate on morality and civil life and a more urbane tolerance for diverse styles of life. Others may take the long-term outcome as more problematic and see in the succeeding debate the possibility of so much confusion that coercion rather than tolerance may be the effective resolution. Yet, as Irwin points out, past urbanization has generally been accompanied by such tolerance and while the present diversity of lifestyles and social movements may strain people's patience, the Western urban aspiration has been one of tolerance balanced by self-imposed restraint.

What is essential, of course, is that the urbane ethic of tolerance be reciprocal—that one be willing to settle for a plurality of urban scenes rather than insist on the righteousness of one's own. While such a resolution affords great individual freedom, it abandons any compelling moral claim that one's own style of life is worthy of evangelical zeal. This urbane—indeed, blasé—extension of reciprocal tolerance can be seen as deadening and without passion, another step toward the "disenchantment of the world." Here Irwin takes a different and novel turn, arguing that while such reciprocal tolerance may represent a philistine void to the intellectual, it can also represent an expressive feast to the urban masses. The new liberties—providing they are contained by self-imposed limits—do provide a widened range of personal expression. It is not just that each group can till its own garden, but that there are more gardens to be tilled.

In this respect, it appears to me that Irwin's perspective on this period moves in a direction that is different from those who have taken either a charitable or uncharitable attitude toward the most prominent movements of the recent past. For some, the upheavals of the last decade and a half are a noisy disclaimer to the end of ideology. For others, they are merely the death throes of chiliastic antimonism, knee jerk monstrosities, academic prophesies, or mini-ideologies which provide straws for grasping moral zealots. For both sides to this debate, the "New Left" is the most general term which is available to caption the whole period. Such a political label, however, captures only a slice of what went on during most of this period, and in Irwin's view it is scarcely worth mentioning. Such a difference is perhaps expectable since sociologists seldom got to the beaches or crash pads, but for the most part looked at student demonstrations outside of their office windows. For them, it was a political confrontation, and for both students and faculty that seems to be the idiom in which confrontations are possible.

In Irwin's view, most of the action was not on campuses, and politics played a subordinate role in shaping the content of these urban scenes. In large part, they were simply new forms of self-expression, group indulgence, and an incorporation of new people into the cosmopolitan life of metropolises. One can dismiss it as "consumerism," but in large part it is a kind of consumerism that most of us accept when we ourselves practice it.

As Irwin points out, this expansion of self-expression extended to include many groups—youths, blacks, welfare recipients—who had previously been expected to demonstrate exceptional shows of asceticism. The real question is whether or not we can stand these new shows of self-expression and consumerism on the part of populations that we once thought of as rather abject and humble. The New Left and its attendant ideology were certainly important elements in shaping public attitudes and responses, but focusing too narrowly on this element misses the expressive, consumptive main thrust of many of the groups that emerged alongside the New Left. Indeed, the central issue to surface during this period may not be the renewed eruption of evangelical political doctrines, but the more durable problem of tolerance in an increasingly heterogeneous urban society.

In this respect, it seems to me that Irwin is more nearly a disciple of Simmel than of Weber. For Simmel, the city housed so many styles of life that the blasé attitude was the only reasonable attitude. For Weber, the disenchantment of the world was a dark prophecy and without redeeming virtue. As Irwin sees it, however, the blasé attitude is what protects the variety of urban life and allows us to enchant a small corner of it, if not the entirety of it.

—Gerald D. Suttles
University of Chicago

Introduction

In undergraduate and graduate schools, I attempted to penetrate the vague and esoteric abstractions of sociology. Like most students, I kept searching for concepts which my own social experiences embodied. At 16, I had been an incipient "hot rodder"; at 17, a "hoodlum"; at 18, a "head"; at 19, a would be "safe-cracker"; at 20, a "construction stiff"; at 21, a "thief" (again); at 22, an almost "dope fiend"; from 23 to 28, a "prison intellectual"; and at 28, a "surfer." These were all well-known collective pursuits which were available to be tried by myself and my peers. When many of us plunged into them—which we did gleefully and some of us did voluntarily—we understood that we were not making an exclusive or lifetime commitment.

I know that my biographical listing is an extreme one; and that Los Angeles and California, where I grew up, are different from the rest of the country—but the list is not that extreme, nor is the place that different. For instance, as Claude Brown in *Manchild in the Promised Land* and Piri Thomas in *Down Those Mean Streets* described their youth in New York, the same general awareness of multiple collective enterprises and flexibility in commitment appeared. From my point of view, my generation in Los Angeles and some large portion of young people in cities all over the United States lived in a society made up of multiple pursuits ("worlds") like those listed above, to which we related with a great deal of flexibility, choice, and delight.

Sociology in the late 1950s and early 1960s, when I was learning it, had no understanding of these worlds or of this type of commitment. Of course, none of the standard concepts, such as primary group, secondary group, social system, social structure, social class, or formal organization came close. Some work in the field of deviance was slightly better,

17

but gangs, subcultures, and behavior systems did not approach the casualness of the worlds I was involved in. All such gangs and subcultures suggested too much commitment, determinism, instrumentality, and stability in membership; they failed to catch the essential dimension of the social enterprises in which I participated—that is, enterprises with the quality of being well known to a large circle of people involved in and witnessing certain activities. Concepts such as milieu, ambience, fad, and craze, on the other hand, did not suggest enough permanence, cohesion, or complexity of form. The concepts which came the closest were "reference world" or "social world," as developed by Tomatsu Shibutani in 1955. He recognized that mass communication made it possible for people to identify with reference worlds or social worlds from a distance, and also noted that they could identify simultaneously with different worlds, so that many of these worlds had loose, even fictitious memberships.

His treatment was on the right track, but incomplete. I finally realized that what Shibutani described was an emergent *urban* phenomenon and would have to have a new analysis. Just as I set out to do this, the phenomenon itself progressed to such a degree that ordinary people (as opposed to social scientists) began to label many of their activities as the "scene," "bag," or what one is "into," and began to talk openly about such worlds. I decided to pursue the first metaphor—the scene—which seemed to capture many dimensions of the collective activities, and to reflect essential aspects of the orientation of individuals who "made scenes." This metaphor, a theatrical one, was especially appropriate for me because I am a student of Herbert Blumer, Erving Goffman, and David Matza, all "symbolic interactionists" or "dramaturgic" sociologists.

I have been working on an analysis of scenes for the last ten years. Even in a study of prisons, I treated "criminal behavior systems" as social worlds to which individuals committed themselves somewhat voluntarily. For instance, in 1970, I described the relationship between the felons I studied and their systems in the following manner: "Many persons have contact with more than one system and the systems themselves, because of cultural diffusion, interchange of members, and common background characteristics, are overlapping."

Since that study, I have been engaging in and supervising students' studies of urban scenes and trying to develop an analysis of the emergence and spread of this collective phenomenon and the contemporary social orientation of the "actor."

This book is the end product of all my efforts. In brief, it presents an analysis of a different social entity—the scene—which is spreading through the urban world, and of a new social posture—the self-conscious actor—who regularly manages impressions of self in front of others as in front of an audience. After a brief, preliminary analysis of the social and historical changes which produced scenes, I will look at different types of scenes, their structures and histories (Chapters 1 through 4). Then I will provide a more thorough analysis of the social processes responsible for this absorbing new phenomenon and of the self-conscious actor (Chapter 5).

I will conclude with an examination of the actor's orientation, not restricted to different types of self-conscious acting, but including some of the larger issues related to the plight of actors in our modern urban society.

1 | URBAN SCENES: Leisure Activities

MEANINGS OF THE MODERN CITY

The city emerged, developed, and endured for centuries as a *social machine.* It was primarily a complex instrument doing the collective work of a people or an assemblage of peoples, and it allowed them to increase in size, density, variety, and prosperity.[1] It was especially an economic center where groups traded their commodities for those produced in their own city, other cities, or the hinterlands. It was an administrative-political center where these complex economic activities and other social activities were planned, regulated, and protected. It was also a mystical center where the church and other integrative institutions were located and in which people engaged in symbolic activities that defined and united them. In other words, the city was a place where people joined in the tasks, rituals, and other common activities necessary for them to coexist, survive, and grow as a large complex society. And when the process worked, the *society* survived, grew, and prospered.

The city, or modern urban arena (with cities interlaced until the contemporary society is dominated by their patterns and influences) still accomplishes most of its original societal purposes. It has added many more, such as supplying water and energy, education, health care, welfare, sanitation, and police protection. However, for a growing number of city residents, particularly younger people in modern nations such as the United States, these societal and provider functions are no longer the *primary* purposes of the city. The reasons for this change in emphasis, simply stated, are that in the modern, complex, industrial world, the city (or the urban society) is secularized and demystified; decision-making and social control have become abstract and remote; and economic activity no longer has meanings for *collective* survival. Persons do still come to the city (or continue to live in it) because of jobs, but the modern meaning of a job is not the same as it used to be. Work is no longer seen as a fundamental, collective survival effort; more often, "a job" is merely a hassle endured to provide money—for individual survival, yes, but more importantly for other, mainly expressive and leisure activities. Today many people perceive the city more than anything else as the place one lives in or travels to for these expressive and leisure activities. Now, more than ever before, the city has become an *entertainment machine.* Entertainment is the *new* collective activity, replacing or supplementing survival as the primary concern of urbanites.

THE EMERGENCE OF SCENES

The city has always offered many forms of entertainment. For instance, in *A World of Strangers*, Lyn Lofland describes the rich array of entertainment which was available free to the citizens of the preindustrial city.

> The actors and street singers and story tellers and readers and beggars are out in even greater numbers and are attracting even

greater crowds. Again, if this city is a "Roman" sort of place, you might go to the Coliseum or to the Circus Maximus to enjoy the amusements provided you by the rich and mighty of the city. But if it is not a "Roman" sort of city, the streets and plazas and squares themselves are likely to be turned into places of amusement. Perhaps there is some religious ritual, perhaps the elites will show themselves by parading through the streets. Perhaps there will be dancing or human sacrifice or animal sacrifice or battles between men or between men and animals or between animals. Or perhaps the spectacle will be as simple as watching someone beat a dog with a stick. But whatever there is to be seen, it will be enjoyed with great gusto. And it will be free. [p. 33].

The city has continued to create forms of entertainment in which anybody (usually with the price of admission) may engage. There are movies, restaurants, plays, operas, museums, art shows, sports events, zoos, amusement parks, circuses, dance halls, gambling casinos, aquariums, and Disneylands—each important in the meanings 'of the city to modern urbanites. So important are they that the New York *Times* recently (January 9,1977) acknowledged that the tourist industry was one of the city's main hopes for revitalizing its economic life.

However, there are newer expressive and leisure *social worlds* which are more complex and much more important than mere forms of entertainment in supplying the city and urban world in general with its new primary meanings. These latter "worlds" are the entities I call "scenes." I chose this particular label because it has often been used by laypeople to refer to these activities. Like so many "folk" labels, it conveys many of the essential meanings of these new social worlds.

For instance, the label indicates that these worlds are expressive—that is, people participate in them for direct rather than future gratification—that they are voluntary, and that they are available to the public.[2] In addition, the theatrical metaphor of the word "scene" reflects an emergent urban psychological orientation—that of a person as "actor," self-consciously presenting him- or herself in front of audiences. We will present a more complete analysis of this orientation and some of its consequences after we've thoroughly treated the scenes themselves.

There are immediate reasons why expressive leisure activities have become so important in the lives of modern urbanities, particularly young Americans. First, there has been a loss of central, overriding societal purpose. Second, the general prosperity which followed World War II has actually and conceptually released hundreds of thousands of people from the mundane, "work-a-day" life and supplied them with leisure time and money to spend on expressive, entertaining activities.

Of course, this emphasis on leisure activities is not *totally* new to the city. Certain strata of the city have always been relatively free (or excluded) from "instrumental" activities, and they spent large amounts of time in leisure pursuits. By and large, these strata—the elite and the "demi-monde"— moved outside the main-stream, either above it in a highly privileged position which provided them with the economic resources to devote themselves to leisure, or below it in a position of disadvantage, from which they could not afford, or were not allowed, to take a normal direction in a normal style. In addition, middle-class bohemians, by choice it seems, have stepped out of the mainstream and participated vigorously in leisure and expressive activities. There have been other periods in urbanized America when there were lulls in the national purpose and relative prosperity, during which large numbers of "ordinary" middle-class persons turned to expressive and leisure activities. The "gay nineties" and the "roaring twenties" were such periods.

However, today there is profound and widespread alienation because of the demystification of society and the loss of any clear central purpose that would justify personal sacrifice. An unpopular war and the presidential scandals have deepened this alienation. Add to this the prosperity which has been extended to the majority of society since 1950 and the modern mass communication system augmented by television which spreads news, ideas, patterns, and meanings around the country with unprecedented rapidity. The consequent quality and quantity of leisure and expressive participation is thus new in our history.[3]

One reason for the collective response to the availability of leisure is that individualistic entertainment is not enough to satisfy most persons' inherent, profound need for collective involvement. Human beings are, of course, gregarious. They enjoy—in fact, suffer without—contacts with others to share expressive experiences, chat, dance, shout, play together, touch each other, make love, or generally interact. The contacts are an end in themselves, but to be meaningful they must possess some depth and durability. Entertainment activities attended only by strangers who do not interact or interact superficially and minimally are not enough to satisfy collective, expressive human needs.

The modern city, however, has erected barriers between people. In the highly mobile city, most people one meets, passes, or finds oneself among are total strangers. One has little in common with them beyond the same physical location and, most of the time, the same national tongue. Usually there is not enough trust or shared meanings to get beyond superficial "niceities" or necessary public propriety. Only very rarely is there enough trust or shared meanings to begin satisfying the need for collective activities.

Another way the modern city has placed obstacles between its individuals is that city dwellers have had to learn to function in a constantly crowded world, with required contacts many times more numerous than they were in pre-urban or pre-industrial times. People have been forced to adopt a highly impersonal, particularized mode of interaction, which sociologist Louis Wirth said is "face to face," but which is, according to other sociologists, "nevertheless impersonal, superficial, transitory, and segmental." This mode of interaction is absolutely necessary to make the city work and to allow urbanites to maintain their sanity. An individual in today's city has so many daily contacts that allowing each to have a strong emotional impact would soon be totally enfeebling. Clerks, shoppers, secretaries, managers, or TV repairmen cannot stop what they are doing and discuss their families, their personal problems, their life histories, their future plans; they cannot argue ideologies or individual tastes with all—or even with many—of the persons they contact in the course of a day. They can and do occasionally go beyond the narrow, formally drawn limits of interaction, but they cannot continue to do it and function. They will be fired or go nuts, whichever comes first.

Alvin Toffler in his *Future Shock*, defends what he calls the "modular" relationship.

> In a modular relationship, the demands are strictly bounded. So long as the shoe salesman performs his rather limited expectations, we do not insist that he believe in our God, or that he be tidy at home, or share our political values, or enjoy the same kind of food or much that we do. We leave him free in all other matters—as he leaves us free to be atheist or Jew, heterosexual or homosexual, John Bircher or Communist [pp. 98-99].

Once someone gets used to this modular mode of interacting, however, he or she finds it hard to alter. Persons accustomed to interacting with strangers, in a segmented manner, are very suspicious and ill at ease when those strangers try to establish friendlier and more complete relationships. Therefore, a major problem in the city is finding a way and a place where one may justifiably plug into more complete, emotionally sustaining relationships. The "scene" is more and more a way of solving this problem.

ACTIVITIES

Swirling in and around every large city are hundreds or thousands of leisure, expressive scenes which I will label "activity systems." What each possesses is some central leisure activity or set of activities such as: tennis, volleyball, squash, car racing, juggling, cooking, skateboarding, transcendental meditation, nudism, skydiving, poetry reading, stamp collecting, and countless others. Of course, people still engage in these activities for their own sake and without moving out of private spheres, as when friends play a few hands of bridge after dinner. But each of these activities is the focus of a scene, or numerous scenes.

These scenes are located in public places. Their central activity has been embellished with a set of special meanings, rules, symbols and subsidiary activities which have emerged out of the interaction of the participants. For instance, bridge has its "master's points," "duplicate tournaments," "Schweinwald system," "Jacoby Transfer," and "end play." Many people go to the scene locations to engage in the activities *and* to be among others *and* to meet new people *and* to share the meanings of the scene with friends and strangers. What they are after is not just the enjoyment of the activities, but to become involved in collective expression or "action." To find action, they move on to the public stage, enter the drama, or "make the scene."

Action, which is what people are seeking in the activity systems, has four separate aspects and all activity systems have at least the first—collective involvement, or being among people engaged in a common activity. This in itself is gratifying, as being present when others are engaged in intense activities is exciting to most people. Look at the crowds at the Kentucky Derby or the Indianapolis 500 who cram together in the infield where they will not be able to see much, if any, of the races. Or think of the people who go on nice evenings to the "action" bars on First Avenue in Manhattan or Union Street in San Francisco to stand outside because there is too much of a crowd inside. Or of the people at sidewalk tables on the Boulevard St. Michele or Les Champs d'Elysees who watch throngs of strangers mill by. Joining in the collective activities is even more gratifying. For instance, events such as the early Fillmore dances, Billy Graham revivals, and pro football games are exciting because so many people are moving and shouting *together.*

The second aspect of action is commingling with others for the purpose of making contacts with potential sex partners. Earlier in the development of the awareness of action, Blake Green, a San Francisco reporter, described the "action game" in the San Francisco *Chronicle*:

> And it's the Action Game that pulls them through the swinging doors, up to the barstools, into the tiny booths or standing five deep on the barroom floor. They march in straight from the ladies' room of their offices, their mascara barely dry, running their tongues over fresh lipstick, fingering the blonde or brunette guiches on their cheeks.
>
> And, often in front of them, but at least close behind—like eager bloodhounds on the trail—come the Men in the Gray-Black-Olive Flannel (or Dacron) suits. Out of the sunshine, the drizzle, the fog they come—to stand, to stare and then . . . to make The Approach [May 16, 1966, p. 7].

A third aspect is physical or sensual stimulation, which can come from a variety of sources, such as body motion, sounds, tastes, smells, open sexuality, or "expanded consciousness." Although each person does not seek the same form of satisfaction, we shall assume that all humans enjoy and seek it generally.

The last aspect is risk. Risk breaks into two interacting categories: physical and reputational.[4] Physical risk exists when activities entail some possibility of bodily harm. The action quality is increased when the actor can exercise skillful control over the danger, but some margin must still be left to fate or luck. For instance, race car driving, surfing, skiing, and mountain climbing are all great action activities because both skill and luck are facets of physical risk.

Reputational risk involves some possibility of psychic harm. These challenges may also involve physical danger, such as in the activities referred to above. However, they entail in greater proportion the risks taken when individuals attempt to win love, respect, admiration, or envy by performing or by displaying themselves in front of others. Performances or displays may range from activities which draw the attention of everyone present—acting, dancing, singing, or playing a musical instrument—to much less obtrusive displays—trying to attract one or a few sexual partners. The risk here is that, if the presentation is ill-received, then one's reputation gets tarnished.

In addition to offering action, to qualify as an urban scene, the activity system must be "available." Availability means primarily that knowledge of the activities and of the more obvious patterns and meanings of the scene are disseminated to a large audience of potential participants. Initially, this may be accomplished through word of mouth, but later this availability is communicated through the mass media which, particularly in feature stories and the specialty magazines devoted to a plethora of leisure activities, spread information about scenes widely. Availability also means that there cannot be any inherent or imposed restrictions on participation which drastically limit access to the activity systems. Extreme costs, as in polo, or highly exclusive membership, as in many elite organizations such as golf "clubs," are examples of restrictions which move an activity out of the scene category.

The requirement that they be open or available eliminates from our direct concern many of the city's social activities which are very scene-like. For instance, groups of workers in a work setting engage in expressive, leisure activities during work hours and develop a special meaning world around these. The pattern in exclusive clubs is similar. However, we are interested in meanings and uses of the city for the general population. We will look at the expressive, leisure social worlds which are open to large numbers of urbanites, which are part of the popular culture, and which, we are suggesting, give the city its new meaning.

As with all things, scenes are only more or less distinct from other activities. Many new urban scenes are relatively available. For instance "bowling on the green" in New York's Central Park is known about, but it tends to have a small membership exclusive to the elderly and retired:

> Bowling on the green, one of the more genteel ways for a sportsman to work up a perspiration, had returned to the park, as it has every year since 1925: gracefully.
>
> From now until December, the lawns just off the park's West Drive at 69th Street will be used by lawn bowlers on Tuesday, Thursday and weekend afternoons. The approximately 100 bowlers, many of them retired, belong to a loosely organized club that pays the Parks Department a fee for the use of the 120-foot-square lawns.
>
> "This game is the friendliest game there ever was," said Anton Diebold, the group's president, adding: "This is very important in New York. So many people are lonesome. This cements friendships" [New York *Times,* May 6, 1974, p. 39]

We will concentrate on the more available scenes.

When all these qualities are present—a central leisure activity, a set of special symbols and meanings, relative availability, and action—we have a scene. It is a locale, a stage, where urban actors can voluntarily enter into expressive drama, can put themselves on display to affirm their character, meet new people, take risks, engage in exciting, stimulating physical activities, and converse about the special and subtle meanings which surround the activities. Increasingly, modern urbanites are retreating from serious, conventional pursuits and organizations, from work-a-day life, and seeking these expressive, leisure forms to fill their lives with meaning and pleasure, and to circumvent the barriers the city has placed between them.

PLUGGING IN

But just how do individuals "plug in" to these social worlds? How do novices locate and then become part of the collective activities? First, most scenes provide well-known locations at which participants commingle, act, and share the meanings which are part of the process. Almost every scene has its bars, taverns, coffeehouses, courts, sections of the beach, ski slopes, country clubs, bowling greens, meetings, conventions, parties, or other special locations or situated occasions identified with the activity system. There are prominent participants at these locations or occasions, and newcomers know that they can join with them in order to participate in the activities.

These scene locations can be available regularly and frequently, or only periodically or intermittently. If they are available too irregularly, then usually a communication system—such as a newsletter, a journal, or radio conversations on citizens' band radios—keeps up the interest and commitment to the activity, communicates the meanings of the activity system, and announces the times and places of upcoming situated activities. Take, for example, the Morgan Club of Northern California. The club requires a Morgan car for membership and meets several times a year. Between these meetings, it circulates a regular newsletter tying the participants into the scene. A passage from one of these newsletters, the *Morgazette* of January-February, 1974, demonstrates its functions well:

> 1974 will bring new adventure, thrill, intrigue, and a lot of good times to the Morgan Club and all you MORGANEERS out there . . . We will be embarking on events, this year, that haven't ever been done before . . . as well as to bring back those tried and true events taken each year. Out of the annals of Morgandom, dusted off and reborn each year to ever enliven these hearty Morgan Souls . . . Some of the trips will include: A trip to Hearst Castle in early summer, the Mother Lode tour (we hope to make it to Harrah's auto collection again this time, weather permitting).

Mendocino and Gus', some South Bay wine touring, and much, much, more.

In addition to situated activities, it is possible to meet other actors in one's scene at places which are not special locations, because actors in a scene tend to wear similar "costumes." Because dress styles overlap or change rapidly, however, they are not highly reliable scene identifiers, although they often serve as initial sensitizers to the possibility that strangers share a common dramaturgical world. A few exploratory questions sometimes sprinkled with argot quickly determine if this is so. Such statements as "Do you play duplicate?" "Do you dig salsa?" or "Do you know the hustle?" will quickly and more specifically identify people whose outward appearance hints that they may share an interest in one's scenes.

Once such initial contact is made, being around the activities and around others who are engaged in them will often furnish one with the necessary skills, meanings, values, and language to get by as a participant. With some time and effort, one becomes a full-fledged scene actor. For, with minimal economic, age, or racial restrictions, scenes are remarkably permeable, their main requirement being that the actor is willing to take seriously the drama of the scene.

SELECTED SCENES

FERN BARS: THE NEWEST BAR SCENE

All discussions of urban leisure patterns in America must begin with bars, since these are the most frequently used and most available urban scene. Their problem is that they are *too* available. The role of the activity system is to supply a situation for urbanites in which they may become involved with others in some common activity—preferably, an intense collective one. This allows persons to experience the rewards which come from collective involvement, to engage in exciting activities for their own sake, and to meet new people for satisfying interaction, friendships, and, perhaps, sexual relationships. But the heterogeneous city is crammed with different types of people, of whom many are antagonistic, incomprehensible, repulsive, or threatening to each other. If the mechanism which pulls them together is going to be successful in promoting shared activities, it must either pre-select relatively compatible individuals or provide techniques for participants to select from the individuals present those with whom they will enter into more enduring relationships. There are "home territory" bars, which attract a particular crowd of persons who share some characteristic or characteristics (such as living in the same neighborhood, or being gay); in these cases, the clients and management discourage outsiders from using "their bar." We, however, are interested in the more open activity systems, and thus the home territory bars lie just outside our direct focus.

With regard to being able to provide participants means to select those with whom they want to interact, bars in general rank relatively low. To some extent, all who walk through the door open themselves up to engagement by all others present. Sherri Cavan, in a study of bars in the 1960s, entitled *Liquor License*, emphasizes this aspect of public drinking places.

> Public drinking places are "open regions": those who are present, acquainted or not, have the right to engage others in conversational interaction and the duty to accept the overtures of sociability proffered to them. While many, perhaps the majority, of conventional settings customarily limit the extent of contact among strangers, sociability is the most general rule in the public drinking place [p. 49].

There are some very sedate bars, in which separation of clients is the rule, and there are some techniques (such as sitting in a corner of the room, or staring straight ahead and not talking to anyone while sitting at the bar) which are somewhat effective in maintaining distance from others present in most bars. However, inebriation tends to weaken commitment to the informal rules of public privacy which make these techniques work; thus, carefully planned strategies to remain aloof usually fail in the bar. So, generally, I agree with Cavan: Bars leave people open to the approach of all others present whether or not they belong in or take seriously the particular scene.

In addition to the problem of screening for incompatabilities, bars in general do not solve the special problems of women who by joining in this activity system seem to automatically make themselves available for sexual relationships. This reduces their capacity to participate conditionally. Women in a public setting and especially bars typically wait to be approached. This creates a problem because they do not like every man who approaches them, and prefer some who do not. In addition, women are more cautious about entering into sexual relationships because they are more likely to be physically and psychologically damaged by men who "pick them up." Even after the "sexual revolution" and women's liberation, men generally are more willing to move immediately to sexual activity, while women prefer to build a broader, deeper relationship first. Men still can "take advantage" of women with whom they have sexual relationships: That is, they can perform the sexual act with callousness, brutality, or general inconsideration of a woman's feelings. Also, they often spread disparaging characterizations of women after sexual encounters. Guarding reputations is important to women because they, still more often than men, lose status when they are labelled such things as "promiscuous" or "bum lays."

A system is needed which minimizes the dangers for women by affording a time period during which women can screen out undesirable men. The more open bars do not offer this system, except to a small group of regulars who attempt to make the bar their home territory and to maintain a small friendship group who are well acquainted with each other.

But for the rest of the clients, and it is they in whom we are more interested, there is little opportunity for screening. Consequently, fewer women than men use bars to meet friends and new lovers.

In addition to the problems the bar creates for women, it is not totally satisfactory for men either. Since women operate with an ingrained set of preferences and fears, they typically turn down many or most men who approach them. The "risks" there are high for men; prestige and dignity among many American males are linked closely with sexual attractiveness and powers of seduction. To minimize the potential humiliation and ego deflation in sexual flirtation, men also need an interactional structure which allows people a graduated introduction. It is safer for men to flirt in casual conversation, where hints or ambiguous offers (often disguised as jokes) can test the interests and attitudes of the other person and the possibilities for future sexual relationships.[5] A good scene provides many opportunities for casual conversation to occur "accidently." In this type of setting, more explicit and "risky" offers can be made after a step-by-step testing process has permitted sufficient mutual assurances to be exchanged.

In the encouraging of this testing, the bar rates no better than "fair." Most bars have rows of stools which allow strangers to be next to each other "accidentally." Thus, occasionally, a man finds himself next to an available, desirable woman; but there are more men than women in the bar, and empty seats next to available, desirable women are quickly filled. This makes necessary more obvious approaches, such as sending a drink through the bartender or approaching a woman or women seated at a table. However, these are definitely explicit offers and make the man vulnerable to a rebuff. This vulnerability works both ways, of course. A woman who makes herself available in the bar activity system and receives no offers is equally humiliated.

An additional serious shortcoming of the bar scene as an activity system is in the nature of its central activities— drinking, and socializing with alcohol as the catalyst. Socializing while drinking is often a rewarding and intense form of expressive behavior, but it has serious drawbacks. The most immediate is the hangover or impaired motor coordination. More serious, however, are the longer-term possibilities of health damage and alcoholism. Still, drinking is of one of the great American pastimes, one of the most widespread forms of expressive, leisure activity, and we must take it seriously.

A new genre of bars which emerged in the late 1960s and early 1970s has overcome some of the difficulties described above and enhanced the bar scene's positive aspects— its congeniality and its potential for sexual encounters. These bars, such as Henry Africa's and Perry's in San Francisco, and Maxwell's Plum and Friday's in New York, are often referred to as "fern bars." They have large, uncovered windows (which allow ferns and other plants to be part of the decor) and are well lighted. They are usually decorated with wood, plants, prints, and old photographs.

Until recently, as Sherri Cavan noted in *Liquor License*, bars tried to prepetuate the night by being closed off from the street. This quality provided the client with a sanctuary from the busy-ness and seriousness of the outside, daytime world and tended to promote the "licentious" or "loose" behavior of the evening. However, when bars took on a "den of iniquity" image, they discouraged many people, particularly women, from using them. In addition, when they were closed off from the street the bars were impervious to inspection from the outside, and people contemplating entering could not see if a crowd was present, or if it was the "wrong" crowd. Many, particularly "unescorted" women, would not make the plunge through the door to be confronted by immediate and somewhat embarrassing withdrawal if they discovered that the setting was not right for them.

In addition, the fern bar's open windows allow for street-watching, which brings the action of the street into the bar and gives clients an activity while drinking and waiting for an opportunity to socialize. In this respect, the fern bar has borrowed from sidewalk cafes, which have long been standard public scenes.

Besides the openess and stylish decor, many fern bars provide flexible, comfortable seating areas which, unlike the booths of many of the old "cocktail lounges," do not close groups of people off from each other, and which, in fact, facilitate cross-group interaction and general congeniality. Many of the fern bars have lounging areas which are more like large living rooms than like bars.

The well-lighted room, with its fashionable interior, tends to attract middle-and upper-middle-class young professionals, people in business, and upper-crust bohemians who more consistently and persistently obey the public standards of propriety; that is, such people less often become troublesome, offensive, or combative while drinking. In addition, such men are defined by many young, available females as good prospects for more permanent relationships, and this, in addition to the pleasant decor and the openness, attracts women into the bar. Consequently, the fern bars have maximized congeniality and "action" and constitute the most successful bar scene going.

"DANCE YOUR ASS OFF": THE DISCO SCENE

The discotheque, a contemporary popular dancing scene, has come back with a rush. In 1975, Frisco Disco, or Dance Your Ass Off, a new discotheque in San Francisco, became the most popular spot in town for a wide variety of young San Franciscans. In New York, young people "flocked" to the Leviticus and other such places and made dancing in discotheques the new "in" activity of New York's late-night entertainment scene.

The resurgence of dancing as an important scene should not be a surprise. Dancing affords one of the few situations in which modern adults engage in spontaneous, vigorous, *physical* activity. We must suspect that the human animal enjoys this kind of behavior; our kids seem to experience so much delight in endless jumping, flapping their arms, running, skipping, and screeching. This inclination does not completely disappear as we grow older; in those instances in which adults, for whatever reasons, engage in vigorous, expressive physical activity, they seem to enjoy themselves just as much.

I find it likely that society, as part of training kids to "act like adults," teaches them to behave noisily and vigorously only in special places at special times—and then it does not provide many. Ken Jenkins, in a *California Living* article on "The Movement Movement," describes well this process of suppression.

> We stop running just for the fun of it. We stop letting out shouts, and belly laughs. We stop looking at the treetops and start walking the city sidewalks staring at the pavement. We begin, somewhere along the line, to "keep a stiff upper lip," to put "starch" in our spines, to speak softly and when spoken to. Our behavior becomes "acceptable" and, in the process, we are cut off bit by bit from ourselves and therefore from each other [p. 20].

Not only are we cut off from ourselves and each other, we are cut off from the excitement of feeling our bodies move vigorously. The city allows us to become physically vigorous in sex, a few sports, and dance—and that's about it.

The urban problem of getting to know strangers in general and potential sex partners in particular was discussed above. So, beyond the intrinsically fulfilling aspect of dancing, it is one of the more frequent bridges across the gap the city places between unacquainted men and women. At the "dance" (the dance here refers to any setting where there are music and people, and it has been agreed that popular dancing will be done), it is very proper—in fact, expected—that people who are not acquainted will dance together. If those asked to dance accept (they may without stigma accept or refuse), then there is an opportunity during or after the dance for further interactions if both parties agree to them. In addition to supplying the spatial and social arrangements for conversation between strangers, the dance supplies a shared intimate experience which helps build ties between them.

Dancing is also a gratifying *collective* activity. Judging from the virtually universal, ritual activities of tribal peoples, rhythmically dancing in unison is an intense and exciting form of collective involvement. The modern popular dance is one of the few, if not the only, activities in which large numbers of modern urbanites voluntarily move together in patterns to music. Under the best conditions, the collective involvement—and the excitement and satisfaction it creates—is extreme. The popular dance, particularly since it leaves considerable space within its patterned boundaries for innovation, supplies constant opportunities for risk-taking. There are occasional dance contests, but even without them, there are constant possibilities for one to make a special effort and draw attention, to put on a show—at the risk of being thought a fool, of course.

If the dance scene has these great potentials for action for young and old, why does it rise and fall in importance? Some of this inconstancy can be explained by referring to the cyclical pattern of fads, a process which will be examined more thoroughly in later chapters. In short, in the modern society, a pattern loses its freshness, and therefore its appeal, after too many people become involved in or accomplished at it. In the case of the latest upsurge in popularity, we can examine some of the conditions responsible for the dance's fresh prominence as indicators of the process as a whole.

One of the most important prerequisites was the decline of the music activity system—the rock scene—which had previously been attracting the majority of young white music devotees. In the early 1970s, rock music lost its freshness and vitality, becoming monotonously repetitive, crassly commercial (Alice Cooper, for instance), and imitative of past styles. The activities surrounding the music had narrowed to sitting or standing around and listening to performances. Dancing, which had promoted friendly and satisfying interaction between strangers, had all but disappeared. The "vibes" had turned bad. In fact, the rock scene had been stumbling along mostly on inertia and teenage support for some time.

In the same period, the early 1970s, cocaine and alcohol replaced marijuana as the most desired drugs. It is characteristic of these two drugs to promote active, expressive behavior, whereas marijuana tends largely to promote passivity.

While rock music declined, black soul music, Latin "salsa," and Jamaican "reggae," all of which are primarily dance music, developed into prominence. By 1973 and 1974, in addition, a form of music existed especially for "discos." The music was rooted in the smooth Motown version of soul music (the Temptations, for example) and lent itself particularly well to dancing.

The final ingredient—essential to an upsurge in popular dancing—was a new dance—"the bump"—which was distinct, complex enough to be interesting, and simultaneously simple enough to be learned and executed by large numbers of people. The charleston, the fox trot, and the lindy hop, for instance, had set off dancing fads in the past. Since the 1950s, there were dozens of dances which have swept through segments of the young, particularly black, population. Most were not sufficiently distinct or they were too difficult and could not be mastered by most people without hours of practice. The twist and the skate were exceptions and provided the dance scene with brief revitalization. Now the bump—and, quickly following it, the hustle—have again accomplished a new, healthy dance scene.

All these parts—the disco music, the potential music enthusiasts not involved in other pop music, and the new dances—were combined in various cities by enterprising young entrepreneurs who recognized the potential for a new disco era. To attract crowds, they also added some of the attractions from the hippie and fern bar scenes: various forms of art and light effects; open windows for easy viewing; and ample space for relaxing, watching, talking, and lounging. The result: "nice" places . . . "I come out to the discotheques to dance, to meet people because most the clubs these days are so nice." . . . where a wide variety of young urbanites are mixing and enjoying themselves:

> Now discotheque dancing seems to transcend social, ethnic, economic and even sexual lines.

> "The gays and blacks can make or break a place," observed a young New Yorker who frequents a number of Manhattan night spots. "If they don't show, it's boring" [San Francisco *Chronicle*, January 16, 1976, p. 21].

SKIING

Another very popular, relatively complete activity system is skiing. Some would doubt that this is an *urban* scene, but the modern technology surrounding it is shaped in the city by urbanites, most of the people who participate in it live in the city, and many of its activities—such as selling and buying ski equipment, ski swaps, and ski shows—take place in the city. The mountain ski resort and the skiing scene are definitely urban appendages.

On the dimension of collective involvement, skiing rates highly. In most of its activities, whether on or off the slope, *crowds* of skiers are involved. They gather—or better, squash—together in cars, buses, trains, and airplanes on their way to the mountains; in gondolas, trams, and lift lines when they get there; on the slopes when they are skiing; and, finally, in the lodges, bars, and other "après ski" spots when they are through skiing for the day. While together, they conspicuously share a multitude of meanings, concepts, and categories. Not only are they all obviously skiers and expected to know something about the sport, but they dress alike or within a narrow range of styles, and they carry with them some of the examples of the highly commercial, rapidly shifting ski technology. Ski equipment, which has large, visible trademarks displayed all over it, is the source of instant and long conversations. "How do you like the Olin IV's?" (a very popular ski in 1975), in addition to the old standards like "Great snow today, huh?" can start a conversation which might lead to skiing together or to permanent friendship.

For exciting physical activity, skiing is unsurpassed. It has the rare quality of presenting almost all persons who attempt it physical stimulation from the outset. Moreover, as soon as practitioners achieve some level of skill (usually after a couple of seasons), they can accomplish a fast, flowing, and rhythmic motion which is just about the penultimate in thrilling physical activity. This rhythmic motion can also be a collective pattern done by several people in a line, following each other, moving somewhat as a unit.

The thrills from physical risk begin instantly. As soon as beginners can remain standing, get on the lifts, keep their skis from constantly crossing and negotiate a few simple turns, they find that they can either safely traverse a shallow ski slope or can turn downhill and go faster than their capabilities permit. This quality of being able to move in that margin between control and its loss, in which skill and luck both operate, never disappears, no matter how skilled a person grows.

Especially, reputational risk exists, since all skiers are part of the audiences at each other's performances. At any time on any slope, people may decide to perform to the audience by attempting something relatively difficult for the general skill of most other skiers present. If they succeed, they draw the admiration or envy of those around; if they fail, they are subject to the quiet ridicule or amusement of other skiers. Beyond these impromptu gatherings, there is a formal network of skiing contests ranging from those sponsored by ski clubs through NASTAR (the nationally organized time trials for all levels of amateurs) all the way to the Olympics.

Skiing seems especially well designed for sexual partners to meet. The sport creates situations in which strangers are placed in close proximity as if by accident and during which interest-testing can occur and humiliation from rebuffs can be minimized. There are ski clubs—even ski clubs for singles—which regularly bring strangers together. In the transportation systems to and from ski resorts and slopes, fellow skiers are forced to commingle long enough for conversations. In the hours after skiing, at the hotels, lodges, bars, and après-ski spots, skiers again commingle, and there are plenty of shared experiences and meanings to build conversations upon.

Skiing's best mechanism for getting strangers together, however, is the chair-lift or T-bar. Most ski resorts use one of these systems for transportation up the slopes. Both require two people to travel together side by side for a trip which takes from five to fifteen minutes. People pair up as they approach the lift, and regularly strangers are thrown together. The standard procedure is for people who do not already have a partner to yell to the crowd in general: "Single!" Another "single" responds with something like "Single here." This is not necessarily a random process though it may always be made to appear so. With a little planning and adroitness, a person can time it so that he or she is brought together with someone preselected, although it can still appear to be accidental. Then the long ride up the mountain allows enough time for initial inquiries into the possibility for future interaction. The return journey can and usually does involve regular stops along the way and can, if the two people are willing, permit more interaction. This routine also permits graceful, unhumiliating separations, since the person who wants to terminate the encounter has only to ski down the slope without stopping or by stopping in such a way as to make more conversation difficult, and then to avoid pairing up with the other skier again.

This pairing up is not always as subtle as the ideal given above. I heard a ski patrolman yell, "Single, female only!" Several times I have witnessed pairs of young men split up when they come to the lift lines in order to yell single and have a chance of pairing up with a female.

Skiing is an activity that is easily transformed into a scene. It has all the qualities described above: a leisure activity, its own symbols, availability, and risk. It does have three major drawbacks: It is dependent upon capricious weather conditions, it produces broken limbs, and it is damned expensive.

"GETTING IT TOGETHER"

Tom Wolfe referred to the 1970s, in a recent *New West* article, as the "Me Decade" because of the proliferation of collective (and often highly commercial) enterprises for the purpose of making the self more "centered," "together," successful, or just happy: "T" groups, TM, meditation, EST, Primal Scream sensitivity groups and the like. From our perspective, these activities constitute another activity system which supplies individuals with forms of action similar to the other scenes we have described. This is not to suggest that the stated objectives of these enterprises—that is, of "getting it together" or self-discovery—are not real or important. Urbanization and its concomitant processes have removed or excluded many if not most urbanites from the previously more static and secure traditional social structures. In those structures, they had been embued with relatively permanent, cohesive, homogeneous, and often mystical systems of beliefs, values, and symbols and definitions of themselves. In addition, we recognize that the stepped-up mobility, economic fluctuations, and generally rapid change in the modern industrial city continue to wrench many urbanites loose from more secure niches—such as marriage and careers—into which they have submerged themselves in order to avoid those very uncertainties.

We must also recognize that many people wander through the modern, heterogeneous city with residual values and beliefs from pre-urban cultures, or emergent values and beliefs from new humanist or utopian ideologies. These people experience guilt or pain when they witness, are encouraged to engage in, or actually join in practices inconsistent with those values. For these reasons, and others, we are not surprised that increasing numbers of people have "identity crises" and feel psycholgical pain caused by modernization and its consequent alienation.

But one need not be in drastic mental straits to find in these popular therapies another urban scene—some place to commingle, learn and exchange a set of special meanings and symbols, and take reputational risks. As a matter of fact, one may be in much psychological distress and still seek the collective involvement and the other forms of action as well as the therapy. Indeed, one reason for the popularity of these scenes may be that they provide a relatively controlled and scheduled form for action especially in regard to reputational risk, which in the popular therapies involves more structured routines of self-disclosure. They provide as well an ideology that elevates them beyond mere entertainment and gives them some instrumental aim. In addition, they may appeal to some persons because they need not involve relations that go beyond the present scene. These attractions, of course, are also limitations for the person who is searching explicitly for friends and fun. Maybe this is one of the reasons that these popular therapies have gradually changed over the years from intense, group-centered, professionally supervised efforts at self-disclosure (e.g., T-groups) to more amateurish, self-initiated efforts (TM and meditation).

In any case, "getting it together" is a burgeoning scene which offers "action" to many bored and lonely urbanites, as well as therapy for the identity crises and other psychological problems urbanization has precipitated or aggravated.

THE BOOB TUBE: THE PSEUDO SCENE

In spite of these and other expressive scenes in and around the city, television watching endures as the most prevalent leisure activity in America. Thus, I would like to give some space to a brief discussion of it here insofar as it relates to the type of urban scene we have been exploring. Television is a very convenient and inexpensive pastime; it takes place in the home, and it can be easily enhanced by family values. Much of its appeal, however, springs from the fact that it is a *pseudo scene*—that is, it satisfies vicariously many of the needs and desires that actual activity systems satisfy.

This is not accidental. Writers and producers of television shows purposely construct illusions of action on the screen. There are many mechanisms operating to make viewers feel part of a vast audience "out there in televisionland" and, thereby, to create for them a sense of collective involvement. Constant referrals to the audience, dubbed-in laughter and applause, and studio audiences (there ostensibly to give performers live spectators) all serve to create an illusion of audience participation for the home viewers. Frequent TV polls and the Nielson rating system also give viewers a sense that they are part of a responsive audience. To some extent, consequently, isolated television watchers experience being part of an all-pervasive phenomenon, responding together to television shows. In fact, this is virtually the only urban scene which gives Americans a sense of *national* collective involvement.

In addition, television's prevalent themes of violence and mystery vicariously involve passive viewers in exciting, risky activity. There are obviously intentional production ploys to heighten this sense of involvement—such as giving the audience time to answer the next quiz question or to solve the Ellery Queen mystery. Television can also purport to promise exciting sexual encounters, particularly through commercials selling products which suggest future sexual success.

Television does supply a great deal of material for collective, expressive interchanges in later, actual activities. Discussions among employees and in other situated groups can well originate and revolve around recent television shows. Thus, TV gives people some shared experiences and meanings to talk about. Moreover, sometimes large groups gather to watch a television show—usually a sports event—and actually experience collective involvement with television as the central activity.

Television is related to urban scenes in other ways. Many of these will be explored in a later chapter. We will especially look at the way television seems to provide both the model for what is going on "out there" and a lure to re-create the theatrical in one's life. It is difficult to imagine most of the new forms of scenes occurring without the model and sponsorship of such an entertainment form. Over and beyond these linkages to urban scenes, television operates as a "pseudo scene," a thoroughly vicarious way of seeking companionship, risk, and self-dramatization, all without facing the risks and discomforts of going out into the city to find real action.

CONCLUSION

We have been describing one type of scene. In the remaining chapters, we will look at other types, at the historical and social changes which have ushered these scenes into prominence, and at the situation of the "actor" in the modern city. Before proceeding, stop and consider the broader meanings of the spread of these expressive, leisure activities. All this may reflect that the common culture is evaporating into fragments of personal choice, that people, in rejecting the inflexible, ready-made scripts, are incapable of supporting a national normative system or making the sacrifices necessary to maintain a society. Collective living demands sacrifices—little sacrifices most of the time and big ones on some occasions. But sacrifice has lost its specific connections—its connections to one's career, to one's parents' well-being, to one's neighbors, and most especially to one's nation during its times of war, unemployment, and inflation.

In spite of these indications of a Roman-like decline in today's world, I remain optimistic. In the first place, it is not clear how much consensus or how much "society" is necessary. To some extent, the importance of these has been exaggerated for the purpose of maintaining an exploitative status quo. In the second place, I predict that people will regain enough of their taste for work and sacrifice and their commitment to society and others. These will not be based on taken-for-granted obligations. It is not likely that people will ever again follow the societal scripts because they are "suppose to," or because their parents and leaders tell them to. They have been disappointed too often. The last 35 years of global disasters have revealed to them that national purposes are often ill-conceived. The exposés of the private motivations of presidents and other high government officials have convinced them that leaders pursue selfish goals at the expense of the public good. Many people have followed recommended routines of work and self-denial and still failed to achieve personal goals. The willingness to work and sacrifice for the good of others and for one's own future will come when the connections between these "instrumental" activities and the positive outcomes are clear and probable. In the meantime, the expressive side of the human experiment will remain dominant.

These scene activities are not totally trivial or irrelevant.

Action in scenes is composed of basic human themes. Seeking collective expression, proving oneself in front of others, engaging in exciting physical and sensual activities are as much a part of the human experiment as hard work. As a matter of fact, in many periods in western societies' recent history, particularly early phases of the industrial revolution, it was drudgery that was carried to *abnormal* extremes.

Scene activities are not irrelevant because if the societies of the future are to survive in a world which is rapidly being shrunk and damaged by technology and overpopulation, and if they are to preserve values of freedom and individualism, their citizens will have to be capable of coping with heterogeneity and change, and of negotiating new values and rules for changing situations. This will require a heightened capacity for voluntary action and the skills of mixing with strangers. Scenes, which may at present seem excessively hedonistic, are helpful preparations for this future mode of behavior.

2 | URBAN SCENES: Lifestyles

Our contemporary American urban society has been fragmented. Work has been devalued as a meaningful and essential human collective endeavor; society and its institutions have been demystified; most contacts between persons are specialized and impersonal, and people's lives are divided into little compartments; most people have more material wealth and leisure time than ever before. These factors have created another problem which many urbanites are trying to solve with a different version of the scene.

There is a recognized universal human need for a collective life design to supply individuals with categories for interpreting their surroundings and their interaction with others, with patterns for choosing and acting according to an overall plan, and with career paths through life. Unlike ants, humans do not have a single life plan locked in their genes, nor do they have the capacity to continue without one, responding in an ad hoc manner to each new situation. There are convincing arguments and considerable evidence that human beings suffer confusion, become despondent, commit suicide, develop neuroses or psychoses, or search "desperately" for an identity and lifestyle because they do not possess a collective life design. (A considerable amount of the sociological literature since 1951 has dealt with the individual problems which result from the absence of a collective design.) This design for living was formerly supplied by the family, community, church, schools, or other "traditional" institutions. However the socializing and acculturating efficacy of these institutions has been reduced or diminished to the vanishing point in the modern city.

There are a few notable exceptions and these reveal a great deal, as exceptions, about the general trend away from traditional institutions. In many lower- and working-class urban neighborhoods, such as "little Italy" in Manhattan, the "north side" or "south side" in Boston, and "Chinatown" in San Francisco, there are "ethnic enclaves" in which distinct ethnic groups have preserved many of the characteristics of the small preindustrial, pre-urban community, so the socializing and acculturating functions of the family and the community can still proceed relatively effectively. These ethnic enclaves are more likely to persist in the modern city when there is systematic discrimination against a particular immigrant group and when the native language is still spoken by many of the residents in the neighborhood. Scott Greer, in *The Emerging City*, enumerates three ways in which these enclaves serve the members of the community.

> The [ethnic] neighborhood is greatly strengthened as an interactional scene by its competitive advantage—the native language is spoken here. It is strengthened also by the likelihood that the relatives and friends will live close together, as compared with the vast distances of the metropolis. (Firey tells of one apartment house in Boston entirely populated by paisani from the same village in Italy.) Segregation, in turn, provides a stable and predictable base for a rich maze of voluntary organizations; those brought from the old county, those developed for the purpose of bridging the gap between cultures, and those adopted from the dominant American society [p. 130].

However, as Greer also notes, these neighborhoods are

becoming less important. The children learn English and, in fact, lose their taste for or ability to speak the "old" language. Young adults move away from the neighborhood to seek work and opportunitites. Older members grow prosperous and move to the suburbs where they can get more space for less money. And the enclaves also come under attack from newer immigration and from urban renewal.

In the rest of the modern city—the areas not occupied by ethnic groups—the family still exists as the most common social unit of participation, but it is mainly the nuclear family and not the extended family. Formerly an extended family tied individuals into a larger web which expanded to the community and its churches, schools, work, and decision-making structures. Moreover, this social web satisfied the human need for a design for living by providing the individual with a culture which was "internalized" quietly, inevitably, and almost exclusively by all new members of the society. City dwelers still have some contact with members of their extended family and rely on them for help. However, after they "leave home," they contact uncles, aunts, cousins, and nephews—even brothers and sisters—less frequently and usually not enough to sustain a family-based culture. They have not become absorbed to any extent in a network of voluntary or involuntary "secondary" organizations that would tie them into a larger network which could sustain a single national culture. Research during the 1950s and 1960s revealed that most people living in the city do not attend church, union meetings, political, or other formal organizations even as often as once a month.[1] People growing up in the city today do attend *more* school than rural or pre-urban people, but the modern elementary and high schools have too many students from too many backgrounds to impart and maintain a single cohesive life design. What many, perhaps most, younger urbanites receive from their contacts with the society's traditional institutions is a jumble of partial, contradictory, and apparently obsolete designs for living.

But they have not abandoned the search for a design.

The human need for some cohesive culture is too deeply ingrained. Today more and more urbanites turn to new emergent social entities to supply them with a collective design in much the same way as they offer new bases for collective involvement. As in the case of activity systems, these entities have been referred to by many laypeople as scenes, and it is again an appropriate label.[2]

HOW DID LIFESTYLE SCENES APPEAR?

Lifestyle scenes followed the appearance of the activity system—in fact, they grew directly out of it. We can learn something by tracing this growth. In many activity systems, which were first referred to as scenes—such as the "jazz scene" and the "drug scene"—more and more people who joined stayed on as full-time participants. (Some of the scenes' central figures seemed always to have been full-time actors.) Jazz musicians, for instance, and hustlers, pimps, serious artists, and fully committed bohemians lived the major 1950s activity system scenes 24 hours a day. The late 1950s saw more and more people—disaffiliated from other social organizations, such as work and school, and from traditional institutions—beginning to group around the full-time scene performers. Eventually the activity systems grew into full-time lifestyles for more people than just the scenes' central characters.

This progression was not without considerable tension. The "hangers-on" were viewed with some contempt by the true insiders, and therefore it was difficult for nonessential members of the scenes to create legitimate, full-time places for themselves. For example, people hung around jazz scenes and jazz musicians and tried to be "hip," but because they were not involved directly in jazz, they were tolerated rather than liked or accepted by the jazz musicians. Terry Southern, in an *Esquire* short story entitled "You're Too Hip, Baby," catches this relationship when he describes how Buddy, a black piano player, devastatingly "puts down" a white, non-musician Ph.D. student at the Sorbonne, after he spent months trying to figure out just why Murray had attached himself to Buddy and his wife.

> "Listen, Murray," he said, wiping his hands and sitting back, putting his head to one side, "let me ask you something. Just what is it you want?"

> Murray frowned down at where his own hands slowly dissected the piece of croissant as though he were shredding a paper napkin.

> "What are you talking about, man?"

> "You *don't* want to play music," Buddy began as though he were taking an inventory, "and you *don't* want . . . I mean just what have we *got* that interests you?"

> Murray looked at him briefly, and then looked away in exasperation. He noticed that Jackie was talking to the patron who was standing near the door. "Well, what do *you* think, man?" he demanded turning back to Buddy. "I dig the *scene* and the *sounds.*"

> Buddy stood up, putting some money on the table. He looked down at Murray, who sat their glowering, and shook his head, "You're too hip, baby. That's right. You're a *hippy.*" He laughed. "In fact, you're what we might call a kind of professional *nigger lover*" [p. 124].

The terms hipster and hippie were used derogatorily to refer to the first "groupies" who surrounded the first scene "makers" and who stubbornly tried to create an alternative lifestyle for themselves.

These hangers-on finally succeeded only by generating or joining lifestyles which did not require special skills or talent. These were the "beat," "surfing," and "hippie" scenes. I include surfing hesitantly because at first established surfers did try to keep surfing skill as a requirement for membership. But the influx of thousands of youths into the surfing scene brought down the skill barriers. The other two—the beat and hippie scenes—were designed for ordinary people with nothing outstanding to offer. It is interesting that the last of the three took the name "hippie," which had previously been used as an insult directed at the people who where "too hip"—too obviously trying to become part of a particular scene.

The concept of a scene translated to a whole round of life in which multitudes of unconventional, disaffiliated actors performed. Therefore, by 1967, James Real, a journalist for the San Francisco *Chronicle*, could use the concept in its expanded form when he described the post-army activities of a hippie who had come back to California to join up with "the Scene, and dabble in mysticism, drugs, and communal living." The concept reached rull maturity when the hippies and others around them started referring to all different walks of life as scenes. A colleague of mine was convinced *that* process had occurred in a conversation with his young brother, who had briefly been a hippie. In discussing future plans which were somewhat up in the air, the younger brother stated, "Man, I don't know what I'll do next. I've tried the school scene, and I don't like it. I've tried the work scene and the family scene, and I don't like these either."

HOW LIFESTYLE SCENES WORK

It's my contention that more and more modern urbanites recognize and then embrace lifestyles of real or postulated groups. These lifestyles not only contain the bare outlines of an overall life design, but also a world view, an identity for the individual member, a repertoire of values, beliefs, and tastes, and a set of guideposts for deciding particular acts and future career paths. Since we've seen that the old acculturating institutions have lost their influence, we must explain just how many urbanites become acculturated into these new forms.

To do this, we must start with a new genre of urban "actors." This concept, *the actor*, is especially appropriate for the human being in our scheme, and one which has been developed for us by sociology. Actors, while having been uprooted from traditional institutions, have more knowledge of the world, get around more, and are more cognizant of the fantastic varieties of life around them than were the members of former extended families. They are "relativists"—that is, they are aware of the cultural diversity in their worlds, and they do not believe that their own culture is *the only* culture.

We must also postulate that they have highly developed skills of generalization. Human beings have always been able to take a few observations and, with their language skills and intellect, to form a category out of them. Modern actors have refined this skill and directed it toward taking bits and pieces—a value here, a pattern there, an item of clothing, a phrase or two, a sketchy description by a journalist—and fitting them all together into a real or imagined collective lifestyle.

This talent for generalization is made possible by the same processes which made people aware of the presence of scenes, aided in the corrosion of their traditional institutions, and embued them with their relativistic perspective. These are the information-disseminating systems in our modern society, particularly the mass media. The world is saturated with television, movies, and other forms of communication, and it has become one in which subcultures float, not in the air, but in the ether of the media. Our subcultures have become detached from specific groups, at least in the manner in which they are perceived by outsiders. Tamotsu Shibutani, in a 1955 analysis of subcultures (though he did not call them that), suggested that persons formed conceptions of and identified with reference worlds or *social worlds* (for our purposes, these terms will be synonymous with subcultures) which are not tied to any particular collectivity or location.[9] They are able to do this, Shibutani argued, by selecting pieces from the mass communication channels and fitting them together into a perspective of some imagined or actual group.

Any sampling of the modern media will give abundant evidence that this is possible and is occurring. Most movies attempt to construct a social world as a backdrop for interesting sequences of events in the lives of particular persons. During a single month in 1974, I saw five films, all of which sucessfully constructed different subcultural backdrops: "American Graffiti" created the world of the 1960 teenagers; "Mean Streets," young Italian adults in Manhattan's "Little Italy"; "The Paper Chase," first-year Harvard law students; "Heavy Traffic" (a cartoon), a sordid, urban demi-world; and "Bang the Drum Slowly," professional baseball players. I learned something about the patterns, beliefs, and values of each of these social worlds from the films.

Good fiction and nonfiction have done this for centuries. Quality literature, however, has never reached the audiences that movies or television presently do. Television shows convey descriptions of varied lifestyles in smaller packages than do movies, but they do it more often, in both the program content and the commercials.[3]

Advertisers in general attempt *not* simply to sell products, but to disseminate and popularize images of lifestyles inherently involving the consumption of material things. They present a configuration of appealing "items" among which their own products happen to nestle. The items can be beautiful girls, handsome men, exciting activities, "gusto," relaxation, travel, fast cars, and yachts. The advertisers' products are made to seem essential to the lifestyle, but the lifestyle is really what is being sold.

Playboy is a leading case in point, and the page which *Playboy* formerly devoted to potential advertisers epitomized it. For instance, the monthly ad titled "What Sort of Man Reads Playboy?" in the October 1973 issue displays a "ruggedly" handsome man, dressed in a stylish suede jacket, with a "gorgeous," attentive woman on either side. The three are seated at a crude, but elegant Spanish Colonial table on which there are a handmade copper coffeepot and plates, and three delicious-looking salads. The people are holding wine glasses and seem engrossed in conversation. In the background is a third woman looking at the man with envy. The caption below the picture reads:

> A young man discovering the new trends that eventually become the "now" trends. When he picks up on a new food or drink idea, a new place to travel or a new product to try, others soon follow his suit. And one magazine keeps him informed and helps him set the pace. Fact: more men spend money to read each issue of PLAYBOY than is spent for any other magazine in the world. Want this active, adventurous audience to discover you? Put yourself in PLAYBOY [p. 83].

Newspaper and magazine reporting also play an important role in distributing information about different subcultures and thereby in objectifying these into recognized styles. They do this in special feature or human interest stories (which are, in a sense, journalistic versions of social scientific ethnographies). Many of them are quickly written, superficial, and inaccurate, but, irrespective of their quality or validity, have the effect of spreading information about the heterogeneous world and promoting "lifestyle" as the most recently recognized social form.

Finally, the media have helped crystallize lifestyles into recognizable entities and have elevated them to prominent social forms by attention on celebrities. Orrin Klapp, in his treatment of "seekers," argues that hero worship and cults of celebrities are important directions pursued by identity searchers. He suggests that hero worshippers or celebrity cultists are able, with the aid of the media, to go on "vicarious voyages." Many people today are making such voyages, and many more are learning about distant lifestyles they can emulate, through the media treatment of famous people. This is possible because the media, responding to strong public interest, spend as much or more time and space on the ordinary, typical, day-to-day activities of celebrities as on those aspects of their lives which made them famous. An excellent example of this is the durable and popular "Tonight Show" with Johnny Carson. It has an endless parade of well-known people who talk about their families, their diets, their hobbies, their dogs, and all the other unexceptional details which fill out their lives and lifestyles. The recently introduced *People Magazine* and the television show "Who's Who" are other examples of this phenomenon.

We must emphasize that the styles of life, the perspectives, the potential identifiers carried in the media do not always come across as neatly drawn, sharply focused, or cohesive. They vary from the well-known, rather completely described styles—such as some of the bland, middle American family styles which dominated the "sitcoms" on television through the 1960s—to extremely vague, flexible, dynamic, and ephemeral scenes—like international espionage—of which very few people have anything close to a complete grasp. This often leaves the media audience with the difficult task of selecting from the barrage of material a configuration of items which suits them and from which they can construct a complete lifestyle. Modern urbanites have a growing sensitivity to configurations which constitute lifestyles, and are more or less skilled at this task. The vagueness, the dynamism, and the flexibility of most scenes leave a great deal of room for variation. Still, the less skilled or less informed risk emphasizing values too far from the center of the scene and being considered tasteless and obnoxious by insiders.

The power of the media to disseminate, and the tendency of segments of the public to adopt, lifestyles is demonstrated by the extreme cases in which a "fad" lifestyle appears in one location of the country, is given coverage by the media, and then spreads rapidly to other or all parts of the country. With regard to the emergence of lifestyles in the city, the faddish scenes indicate what is possible and what happens less rapidly in dozens, perhaps hundreds, of more durable, more "respectable" lifestyles. Examples of fads are the New York "bopping" gangs in the early 1950s, California surfing in the late 1950s, and the hippie life in the middle 1960s. I will carefully examine in the next two chapters the full growth of these special scenes.

PLUGGING INTO LIFESTYLE SCENES

In planning what to wear, where and what to eat, what to buy, what to say to others, urbanites keep in mind one or another of the lifestyles into which they are trying to fit. Alvin Toffler describes a young couple selecting furniture and other items.

> The young couple setting out to furnish their apartment may look at literally hundreds of different lamps—Scandanavin, Japanese, French Provincial, Tiffany lamps, hurricane lamps, American colonial lamps—dozens, scores of different sizes, models and styles before selecting, say, the Tiffany lamp. Having surveyed a "universe" of possibilities, they zero in on one. In the furniture department, they again scan an array of alternatives, then settle on a Victorian end table. This scan-and-select procedure is repeated with respect to rugs, sofa, drapes, dining room chairs, etc. In fact, something like this same procedure is followed not merely in furnishing their home, but also in their adoption of ideas, friends, even the vocabulary they use and the values they espouse.
>
> While the society bombards the individual with a swirling, seemingly patternless set of alternatives, the selections made are anything but random. The consumer (whether of end tables or ideas) comes armed with a pre-established set of tastes and preferences [*Future Shock*, pp. 306-307].

Toffler makes it clear in the passages which follow the above that the couple's pre-established set of tastes and preferences are based on existing models which they have gleaned from the media.

The above is just one small slice of the whole process of acting upon a particular scene as a design for living. Persons also shape into a perspective the values and meanings they borrow from the style. They create a world view which contains a slot—an identity—for themselves. They choose a job (when the job market permits), leisure time activities, and a future career plan based on their particular scene. They may even choose a residence according to the scene with which they are identifying. Within a city there are many particular locations, such as Greenwich Village, the East Side, the West Side, the Lower East Side, and Harlem in Manhattan; and the Marina, the Sunset, North Beach, Telegraph Hill, Eureka Valley, Noe Valley, and the Tenderloin in San Francisco in which the residents are more likely to be members of certain scenes rather than others. Outside the city there are layers and pockets of suburbia which represent still other different social worlds.

The lifestyle scene (as does the activity system) offers modern city dwellers settings in which to commingle with others, engage in collective, expressive activities, and establish more enduring social relationships. In addition to the residential areas in which individuals will be among others engaged in a variety of everyday activities, such as shopping, travelling to and from work, and working around the house, each lifestyle scene has a special set of allied activity systems. For instance, many "East Side" New York upper-middle-class "trendies" frequent the East Side "fern bars," play tennis, jog, ski in Vermont, and vacation in the "Hamptons." While "West Side" white middle-class intellectual-bohemians attend off-Broadway plays, ride ten-speed bicycles, and meet for Sunday brunches to discuss the New York *Times* book reviews. As with activity system scenes, mutual participation in lifestyle scenes provides individuals with a pool of shared categories, a set of values, beliefs, symbols, and terms which will allow them to deepen their interaction, once initiated, past the barriers which separate strangers in the city.

CLASSIFYING URBAN SCENES

The nature and importance of urban scenes should become even more apparent after we examine a few of the more prominent examples of these lifestyle scenes. Age and class variables will influence our selection of scenes to explore because these dimensions divide the scenes into natural and recognizable groups. This categorization of life-styles is true in the case of class variables because scenes tend to evolve and remain within areas defined by the values people hold. Members of the working class are less likely to seek out and enlist in middle-class scenes, which they may see as effeminate, snobbish, eggheaded, phoney, or un-American. Middle-class people, on the other hand, more often find such things as baseball, football, bowling, beer drinking, hot-rodding, motorcyclying, or stock car racing vulgar or unin-spiring.

In addition, it seems obvious that access to different scenes is somewhat dependent upon the possession of certain class-related personal attributes and resources (like money). One of the oldest scenes—which used to be called cafe society or the jet set, and is presently called the beautiful people—is only open to those with certain backgrounds or celebrity status and scads of money.

We break our scenes into age grades because age-cycle differences and age-determined relationships to major social institutions (such as education, family, and work) also limit participation in and influence the shape of different scenes. For example, adolescence is a period in which most teenagers are subordinate to two institutions, the family and the school (or their substitute, the juvenile justice system). Conse-quently, it is a period of limited rights and resources. On the other hand, it is also a period of considerable leisure time and a lack of adult responsibilities. We will explore the character-istics of individual age- (and some class-) related differences as we look at various contemporary lifestyle scenes. The brief

descriptions which follow will focus on cultural elements of
the scenes, since, as we have suggested, values, beliefs, shared
meanings, and central themes are the stuff out of which they
are constructed and which make them scenes. Social relationships, material objects, locations, places of residence, and
other components will be included in the descriptions, but
only when they are salient.

CONVENTIONAL LIFESTYLES

TEENAGE: SOSHES AND HOODS

Teenagers have two major concerns. The first is sustaining social relationships with their peers. Teenagers spend a lot
of time in the company of other teenagers and attempt to
move away from the fickle vacillating between being "mad"
and "making up" which characterizes preteen relationships.
The second concern is organizing their emerging, complex
sexual impulses into a viable sexual identity. Other concerns,
such as planning a future career, are totally subordinated to
these two. Out of these conditions emerge styles of social
organization in which values of sociability, popularity, and
sexual acceptability are central.

In the teenage world, high school is very prominent. It
remains so even for "dropouts," many of whom frequent
their old high schools (much to the displeasure of teachers
and administrators) and the high school hangouts, and remain
somewhat oriented toward the social systems generated in
the schools. In the high school milieu, popularity and sociability are major values.[4]

For the past twenty-five years at least, a bipolar status
system has dominated most high schools. The split in this
system is related to the major class division of the student's
parents—between the middle and working classes. The pivots
of the system are two leading figures—variously labelled
soshes, elites, orgs, and bougies on the one side; and hoods,

greasers, bads, vatos, esses, and pimps on the other.

The scene in which the soshes dominate is related to the middle class, and participation in the school-sanctioned enterprises is important. High school athletics and activities—such as being a cheerleader or a football hero—are also very important, as are the high school dances, proms, graduation exercises, student governments, newspapers, and yearbooks. If college is an important goal, which it often is to soshes, then good grades, too, are seen as important.

The value of this part of the system is in being an accepted and recognized member of the "leading crowd." Being an athlete is very helpful for boys. Maintaining ties with other members of the leading crowd through "soshing it up" is of prime importance. The dress, cars, and other material commodities which serve as important status symbols are similar to middle-class material objects. "Malibus," "GTO's," and "Vettes" (Chevrolet Corvettes) were the most popular cars in the 1960s; foreign sports cars have become more popular in the 1970s. Likewise, grooming styles also tend to follow middle-class trends, usually in bolder versions.

The status hierarchy of the sosh end of the system is governed by a combination of characteristics—involvement in school-centered activities, possession of prestige-winning personal characteristics and material goods, proper grooming styles, and, especially, attention to making and keeping the right friends. One of a few leading cliques are at the top, and other friendship groups are distributed down a scale of popularity. Below the bottom of the scale are the people who are oriented toward the soshes, but are sycophants rather than participants.

The other part of the system is analogous to working- or lower-class culture. Participants value being "tough"—that is, willing to employ and confront physical force—or being "cool" or "sharp"—that is, imitating criminals, pimps, hustlers, dope fiends, and other recognized and admired "deviants." As sosh grooming mirrors middle-class styles, the hoods frequently adopt the pimp's flashy dress or the biker's leather and chains. Some hoods have popularized radically modified cars, such as "funny cars," which have huge tires and hiked-up rear ends. Others look at motorcycles as the best vehicles. In larger cities, the prestige car is the "hog" (the Cadillac El Dorado), though few hoods can afford to buy one.

The two opposing subsystems form a bipolar status structure which intensely involves many high school or drop-out youths. The percentage and ethnic makeup of people oriented toward one or the other is, of course, variable depending on the class composition of the students' area. However, in schools with a great deal of ethnic heterogeneity, there tend to be many overlapping systems, instead of a single, bipolar one. In addition, while the bipolar system is a dominant dichotomy, there are many people who do not identify with either prong. These are "outsiders," some of whom maintain their own small cliques and cohesive life-styles (for example, "brains," who strive for good grades and participate in a chemistry club or on a debating team). There have also been occasional incursions into a particular high school system from other scenes—such as the surfing and hippie scenes—which for a time completely alter the school's internal relationships. However, it is most interesting that the bipolar system is an exaggerated, almost caricatured, rendition of the class system in our society, and it is this scene which continues to be dominant for many modern American teenagers.[5]

POST-HIPPIE, BOURGEOIS BOHEMIANS

In San Francisco—as is likely in most large cities—a new lifestyle has emerged among many middle-class young adults whose earlier lives had been touched by the hippie and radical scenes of the 1960s, but who have not continued to openly reject conventional social, economic, and political structures. These people remain profoundly influenced by the 1960s, even though the demise of the hippie and radical movements, coupled with the insecurity of the 1970s, steered them into semi-conventional paths. First, their commitment to society's conventional institutions has been weakened.[6] For instance, they attend school so that they can get a job; they hold a job so that they can survive economically. They, like many of today's modern urbanites, do not rely on these activities to supply their lives with meaning or themselves with identities. Second, they have departed from many of the legal and normative standards of conventional society. For example, they regularly violate drug laws, and many cohabit.

As another result of their radical experiences in the 1960s, they are not as frantically materialistic as their pre-1960s counterparts. They may acquire expensive items—such as sports cars, motorcycles, skis, or stereos—but they value these items much more for the pleasure they get from using them than for their intrinsic value as status symbols. They live in apartments which are filled with old furniture, plants, prints, and posters. Some drive secondhand American cars, VWs, Volvos, Toyotas, Datsuns, or some other economical foreign car. They dress casually—old levis, "earth shoes," and the total absence of suits and ties and evening dresses are presently considered as high in fashion as they care to go.

Beyond this, they drew from the 1960s two important values which are presently fundamental in the structure of their lives. The first is the hippie humanism. It has endured as a general attitude of tolerance and appreciation of others' differences, and a sense of the importance of close, satisfying personal relationships with friends and lovers. The second is a knowledge of the value of spontaneous, expressive, and intense activities.[7] Almost all began using marijuana or other "psychedelics" and found that these helped collective, spontaneous expression. They generally maintain their appreciation of these drugs and continue using them whenever they can.

By clinging to these residues of the 1960s while partially
returning to conventional pursuits, they have constructed a
new scene. According to Craig Reinarman, who studied these
youths (mainly to learn about their cocaine use), this scene
has four major components—a "work trip," "friends, lovers,
and family," "leisure time," and "boogeying."

The Work Trip: Work may be generally defined as those responsibilities and commitments necessary to maintain oneself and
family, not done primarily for pleasure. For the members of the
group, work included formal schooling, formal employment, and
a variety of other activities like painting one's house, shopping, or
fixing one's car. Groups members generally get not great joy from
work activities but feel they must "take care of business."

Friends, Lovers, and Family: Each member of the group spends a
significant amount of time dealing with friends, lovers, and/or
family. Talking on the phone, planning a work or pleasure
activity, or helping a relative or another member of the group
with an errand or problem would all fit into this category, by
default if for no other reasons. These activities involve interaction
with friends, lovers, husbands, wives and children, yet they are
not work as defined here. These daily errands are not leisure
because they require effort, nor are they done primarily for fun.

Leisure Time: Although leisure time is often determined in large
measure by other components which either take priority (work)
or are given priority (boogeying), it nonetheless is built into the
structure of one's daily life wherever it fits. Leisure activities
include a quiet dinner at a home or a restaurant, watching T.V.
and "getting stoned," or crocheting to rock music in one's living
room. Leisure here is used in the classic sense of the term. It is
not work, not necessarily an interaction with friends, although it
often includes "mellow" evenings with a few friends, and not an
all-out pursuit of pleasure. Leisure is something group members
try to maximize, while still "taking care of business," but it is
usually the category most often infringed on by the other three
categories.

Boogeying: The term is used by the group to denote parties, big
nights on the town or spontaneous, pleasurable occasions usually

involving at least three people but often up to 20. Birthday parties, rock concerts, and a night of bar-hopping all fall into this category. Boogeying is perhaps the least frequent and most highly valued type of activity. It is distinguishable from leisure in that the goal is not rest, relaxation, or a mellow good time, but serious playing which normally requires a lot of energy. One of the goals of group members is to boogey as much as possible.

A lifestyle with these components is quite typical of a large segment of post-hippie, middle-class people in their twenties and early thirties. Their cocaine use is incidental. It is a relatively harmless drug which is compatible with the components of the lifestyle and is used with varying degrees of frequency. What is important about this new, very prevalent scene is the four components—outgrowths of the 1960s. The hip middle classes have returned to work or school, but not with the same seriousness of earlier middle-class youths. They may now avoid open rebellion, but they do not fit the mold of conventional Americans. They are passively humanistic and have a relatively large capacity to enjoy expressive, collective activities.

OVER THIRTY: UPPER-MIDDLE-CLASS TRENDIES

In the over 30 age group, occupational and sexual careers have been established (with a wide range of successes and failures). The focus of the life-rounds of those who are relatively successful—in whom we are most interested at the moment—shifts to filling out, embellishing, and refining their earlier directions. Status consciousness, luxury, and privilege, rather than such dimensions as excitement, emerge to shape their lives.

Keeping up with (or ahead of) the Joneses has always been a popular upper-middle-class scene, but it is presently more subtle and complex than it was in the first part of the century. The proliferation of goods after World War II has made yesterday's luxury items, such as expensive cars, available to all of the middle class and a large part of the working class. Wealthy celebrities moved to another level of expensive status symbols, such as designer gowns, private jets, and villas in Switzerland. The primary activity of this lifestyle has consequently become keeping up with the rapidly shifting style and taste *trends*. This involves devoted reading of the journals of taste—*Vogue, Women's Wear Daily, New York Magazine, The New York Review of Books, Gourmet*—and following the purveyors of taste trends—Craig Clairborne (food), Charlotte Curtis (social events), Barbara D'Arey (home decorating), Pauline Kael (movies), and Tom Wolfe ("in" and "out" scenes).

The trends to follow affect many areas, but a lot of them revolve around the home. Trends can involve where to live, what type of home to buy, and how to decorate it. These are not easy choices, and considerable evaluation and consultation with experts are required to keep up with contemporary trends. After all, yesterday's chic is today's gauche.

Of course, the fashion in clothes is important. Presently gourmet cuisine is also very important. But even what to say is important. A cartoon in the *New Yorker* nicely captured the trendie concern over the right thing to say; it showed a woman asking her husband, "I wonder if it is too soon to ask 'what happened to Marshall McLuhan?' "

The primary location for this scene's activities is also the home. House, dinner, and cocktail parties are the major events, for in these, all the status symbols can be put on display. There is the food, from the hot canapes to the white French dessert wine; the decor; and an opportunity for all the trendie conversation.

"Can't you just picture it already, Mrs. Chatfield?" the interior decorator gushes to his enthralled client as they survey the bare living room of her new apartment. "Over there, in that corner, where the sea-ochre walls set off the brindle draperies, I see Tom Hoving talking to Joseph Papp about Shakespeare-in-the-Park. Leaning negligently against the Italian-marble mantel, Philip Roth chats with Susan Sontag about their latest books, while Peter Duchin crosses the room to have a word with Dorothy Rodgers about a forthcoming benefit, plucking a canape from the Regency table as he passes" [*Newsweek*, October 8, 1973, p. 69].

There are several other important extraresidential locations where the trendie activities dominate. Often they are suburban and family-oriented, and as a result, they tend to be more controlled and sedate than the activity settings of other scenes. Country clubs which cater to middle-class people are gathering places for trendies. So are certain resort towns, such as West Hampton or Lake Tahoe. In the city, tennis courts and health clubs, particularly health clubs for women, are often used also.

ALTERNATIVE LIFESTYLES

In rounding out our descriptions of lifestyle scenes, some special attention must be directed toward the *alternative* lifestyles which, after all, preceded the conventional lifestyles in the emergence of scene consciousness and which still exist. The distinctive facet of the alternative lifestyles is that they intrinsically involve patterns which are recognized as illegal or highly unconventional (such as "swinging" sexual activities). Work activities can also be unconventional or illegal. In fact, illegality and unconventionality are especially important because they require the actor joing the scene to consciously "cross a boundary" in order to participate.

DOPE FIENDS

Since the study of deviant lifestyles began in the 1920s and 1930s, sociologists have produced many (perhaps too many) descriptions of alternative lifestyles. One lifestyle that has received a large share of the attention is that of the heroin addict—the "dope fiend." It seems almost unfair to pick on dope fiends again, but I have several reasons for choosing their scene as exemplary of the alternative lifestyles. First, it tends to be one of the more complete, cohesive, and durable scenes—partly because the scene tends to draw people into a secret, full-time, collective routine. Second, there are many good, already existing descriptions to draw upon. Last, most of the previous descriptions have emphasized the negative qualities of the heroin life, and I intend to stress many of the positive facets of a lifestyle which I see as having something going for it.

In an earlier study of dope fiends, I identified four clusters of meanings or patterns which constituted the lifestyle of the drug addict: "getting high," "curing sickness," "not caring," and "hustling, scoring, and fixing."

Getting High. Drugs, of course, get you—in the language of the lifestyle—"high," "loaded," or "straight." Getting high on heroin involves an immediate, overwhelming surge of intense feeling which passes through the entire body, followed by a state of satisfaction that can last for several hours.

We shouldn't be surprised by the importance of this form of intense experience, since the desire for intense experiences is not peculiar to the drug addict. Modern industrialized, rationalized, and routinized adult life has blunted most of our excitement, but dope fiends are in a sense people who appreciate this very special thrill and have developed a whole life around it.

Curing Sickness. The dope fiend considers having his or her sickness cured almost as important as getting high. Alfred Lindesmith, discussing the addict's career in *Opiate Addiction*, emphasized the importance of the initiate learning to define "withdrawal symptoms" and connecting them with the injection of drugs. This is a somewhat narrow conception of heroin as a cure to sickness, however. In the first place, the cure is inextricably tied up with drugs as a peak experience. The drug addict lives in a cyclical pattern, revolving from "high" to "sick," so the meaning of being "high" is to some extent intrinsically linked to being "sick." William Burroughs, in his classic description in *Junkie*, emphasizes the interrelatedness of these two.

> Junk sickness is the reverse side of the kick. The kick of junk *is* that you have to have it. Junkies run on junk-time and junk-metabolism. They are subject to junk-climate. They are warmed and chilled by junk. The kick of junk is living under junk conditions. You cannot escape from junk sickness any more than you can escape from junk-kick after a shot [p. 92].

In the second place, addicts usually see as part of their withdrawl symptoms many ailments which are not directly related to withdrawl. Any physical malady they experience after withdrawing from drugs is likely to be attributed to withdrawal. As one addict who was still complaining of aches and pains after being jailed (and thus drugless) for six months told me, "It takes months to get all that junk out of your system."

Not Caring. Being removed from all care is a category of the drug life that has not received enough attention, despite the fact that it is very important. The best way to convey the meanings related to not caring is in stories told by addicts themselves. The following is one such story from the many I have heard on this subject:

> A lot of times I've gone on the nod in restaurants. One time I ordered some food because I thought I was hungry. But when the chick brought me the food I was going on the nod. Pretty soon my head started sinking down on the counter and my face ended up in the food. After awhile, I guess, I came back out of the nod and looked around. A lot of people were looking at me. There I was with food all over my face. Everyone was embarrassed, but not me. I just wiped off the food with my napkin and sat there. I didn't give a fuck. When you're loaded that shit just doesn't bother you.

Not caring means not being bothered by a wide range of

ordinary, concrete problems, such as financial worries, subjective problems, such as anxiety and neurosis, and everyday interactional problems, such as embarrassment. Dope fiends are impervious, if not oblivious, to these concerns. This feeling of not caring seems to be one of the physiological effects of opiates and, in my opinion, is as important to users as the euphoria. In a sense, the dope fiend has consolidated all the usual and unusual problems of living into one problem—maintaining a habit. As one addict said, "It's like taking all your problems and cooking them up, and sticking them in your arm."

Hustling, Scoring, and Fixing. Finally, one last category of meanings and patterns encompasses the lifestyle of drug addiction. Addicts are typically involved in a daily routine which starts early and lasts on into the night. This routine involves "hustling," "scoring," and "fixing," and to the dope fiend, it is serious business. "The man" (the police) must constantly be outsmarted. The stakes are high—prison if you lose, staying loaded if you win. Though it often comes with pain and discomfort of all kinds, it is seldom dull. As a drug addict described it:

> It is adventuresome to be an addict. Cowboys and Indians at the Saturday matinee didn't have a life that was any more exciting than this.
>
> The cops are the bad guys, you are the glorious bandit.
>
> The chase is on all day long. You awaken in the morning to shoot the dope you save to be well enough to go out and get some more. First you have to get some money. To steal you have to outwit those you steal from, plus the police. It is very exciting.
>
> Now you have the cagey process of converting the stolen goods into dope and when you succeed in all of this you go home and reward yourself for a good day's caginess with a nice big fix.
>
> There are very few vocations offered to me in this society that can be as exciting as the vocation of drug addiction.[8]

When dope fiends "kick the habit," they are faced with the problem that William Burroughs referred to as the "flat world." One drug addict, going through withdrawal at one of San Francisco's drug treatment centers, commented on his chances of staying off drugs:

> I don't have no trouble kicking. I probably kicked more than a dozen habits. It's staying off that gets me. After I'm clean then what do I do. I just can't find anything to fill my time. Any job I can get don't move me. So pretty soon I find myself slipping down to the corner and scoring again.

It's obvious that, despite the drawbacks it presents, the dope fiend lifestyle offers compensations to its followers.

HANGING OUT

While heroin addiction is one of the most cohesive, complete, and frequently described alternative lifestyles, the most common is hanging out. Because it is so common, it is thought of as mundane, and it has not received the attention it deserves. I will try to correct this bias by rounding out this discussion of lifestyles with a description of this pervasive, readily available scene.

THE HANGOUT

Some particular location or small array of locations, known as hangouts by those who use them, are the foundation of the hanging out scene. William Whyte, in *Street Corner Society*, describing the "corner boy," suggests, "Except when he eats, sleeps, or is sick, he is rarely at home, and his friends always go to his corner first when they want to find him" [p. 255]. Hangouts must be places which are available, virtually free, for long hours of the day and night, because their regular users must be able to hang around without spending much money. Hanging out is an indigent lifestyle.

Street corners are the classic hangouts. In two important studies which deal extensively with hanging out—William Foote Whyte's *Street Corner Society* and Elliot Liebow's *Tally's Corner*—the street corner figures centrally in the depictions of the subjects' lives. Other common hangouts are coffeehouses, cafes, bars, bowling alleys, pool halls, and other such establishments located in lower- or working-class districts where people may loiter for hours without spending money. Whyte discovered that corner boys centered "their social activities upon particular street corners, with their adjoining barbershops, lunchrooms, poolrooms, or clubrooms." Liebow offers us another example of a "hangout":

> The Carry-out shop is open seven days a week. Two shifts of waitresses spend most of their time pouring coffee, opening bottles of soda, and fixing hamburgers, french fries, hot dogs, "half-smokes" and "submarines" for men, women and children. The food is taken out or eaten standing up because there is no place to sit down, but in the 10' X 12' customer area, there is wall space and other leaning facilities which lend themselves nicely to the Carry-out's business and social functions.
>
> For those who hang out there, the Carry-out offers a wide array of sounds, sights, smells, tastes, and tactile experiences which titillate and sometimes assault the five senses [pp. 21-22].

REGULARS

The participants in any particular hanging out scene are those who use the hangout regularly and become known to each other. Regulars do not necessarily know any or all other regulars well, but they know some of them on sight and can acknowledge that each other "belong" at the hangout. Patricia Nathe, who studied a bohemian hangout, describes the process of "becoming a regular."

> While a person becomes a regular customer of a hangout, a process of belonging takes place. In a transient shifting society it

is only necessary for a person's face to become familiar enough to engender trust and confidence.

As Elliot Liebow points out, the regulars do not constitute a social group but rather a loose crowd.

Regulars do not work very often or steadily. Hanging out is a full-time lifestyle. Either by choice or circumstance, regulars support themselves by living with other people who provide money, by welfare, "sponging," sporadic employment, unemployment benefits, or, less often, illegal windfalls from such sources as occassional thefts and fees for services rendered to other, more professional criminals (e.g.; habitual thieves, pushers, or numbers men). There are some individuals around the scene who do work or make larger amounts of money regularly, but they invariably only skirt the scene. (The waitresses in the Carry-out mentioned by Liebow are such individuals.) One of the reasons such people must remain outside the scene is that the regulars are usually broke, and any person with a steady supply of funds will be asked constantly for money. A person with an income will be forced to maintain distance while among the regulars, only approach the scene occasionally, or leave the scene for good.

Most regulars in hanging out scenes come from four different social categories: urban working- or lower-class youth (who are labelled and treated as "gang members" because of their hanging out), urban lower-class young adults, white middle-class bohemians, and the elderly.

PASSING TIME

The central activity of hanging out is "passing time." As Liebow noted, a man comes to the corner or the Carry-out "to eat and drink, to enjoy easy talk, to learn what has been going on, to horse around, to look at women and banter with them, to see what's happening and to pass the time" [p. 23].

Conversation is the first basic form of passing time. Nathe found that regulars walk in and out of a hangout several times a day or week looking for old friends or interesting members of the opposite sex to strike up a conversation with. Whether the regular remains or leaves is determined primarily by whether there are people present with whom he or she wishes to converse.

Conversation itself breaks into many different forms, such as "shucking and jiving," "tripping," joking, gossiping, bragging, flirting, "playing the dozens," "mind fucking," "putting others on," "putting others down," "power tripping," "ego tripping," encountering, and reminiscing.

The second basic form of passing time is waiting for action. Hanging out is often monotonous, but this is not because the regulars want it to be. They usually remain available for more exciting expressive activities, such as eating, drinking, "getting high," "partying," "boogeying," dancing, gambling, or any other action which might unfold. However, when no action unfolds, which is often, they pass time waiting for it. Many regulars are remaining available for illegal activities, like the "42nd Street Hustler," whom William Burroughs described so disparangingly.

> This bar was a meeting place for 42nd Street Hustlers, a peculiar breed of four-flushing, would-be criminals. They are always looking for a "setup man," someone to plan jobs and tell them exactly what to do. Since no "setup man" would have anything to do with people so obviously inept, unlucky, and unsuccessful, they go on looking, fabricating preposterous lies about their big scores, cooling off as dishwashers, soda jerks, waiters, occasionally rolling a drunk or a timid queer, looking, always looking, for the "setup man" with a big job who will say, "I've been watching you. You're the man I need for this setup. Now listen. . . ."

In fact, the most common "criminal type" in the country's jails and prisons are participants in hanging out scenes or their close, older relatives—dereliction scenes. Their occasional bumble into felonious crime or this regular engagement in activities such as drug use, street corner drinking, or just plain "hanging out," which are repulsive to other social segments, gets them arrested and even imprisoned on a fairly regular basis.[9]

MAINTAINING FRIENDSHIPS

The last important aspect of hanging out is maintaining friendships. People who hang out on a full-time basis are usually cut off from conventional social organizations. As Whyte suggested, "Home plays a very small role in the group activities of the corner boy" [p. 255]. So it is with other conventional social organizations. The hangout is the only— or certainly the primary—source of social ties. In the face-to-face contacts at the hangouts, the participants construct their social relationships. They become "best friends," "partners," "going for brothers," "lovers," and "ole men and ole ladies." Then they act as if these friendships had a permanence and intensity temporarily surpassing those of conventional social relationships. However, they are maintaining an illusion: Actually, these ties are transitory and fragile. Elliot Liebow comments on the "frailty" of corner friendships:

> As if in anticipation of the frailty of personal relationships—to get as much as he can from them while they last and perhaps hopefully to prolong them—the man hurries each relationship toward a maximum intensity, quickly up-grading casual acquaintances to friends, and friends to best friends and lovers. This rush to up-grade personal relationships, to hurry them on to increasingly intense levels of association, may itself contribute to a foreshortening of their life span, prematurely loading the incumbents with expectations and obligations which their hastily constructed relationships simply cannot support [pp. 217-218].

Hanging out is a scene too often passed over for more exciting deviant phenomena and persistently picked on by the criminal justice system, but it makes up in availability what it lacks in quality. It is the residual scene in urban life. When no other more gratifying or dignified conventional lifestyle is available, and when lack of opportunity, skills, or confidence exclude individuals from more exciting and profitable deviant lifestyles, there is always hanging out. And, as you would expect, more people hang out than engage in any other systematic deviant activity.

3 | The GRAND SCENE

Since World War II, two scenes—surfers and hippies—reached extremely high levels of popularity. At their peaks, they literally involved hundreds of thousands of people. The vast majority of the population knew about them, and their influence extended throughout society. Moreover, the widespread popularity of these two scenes, to a great extent, was responsible for bringing about a more extensive awareness of the existence of alternative lifestyles. Therefore, they helped cultivate a sensitivity and a responsiveness to scenes in general. In addition, the speech patterns, dress styles, and attitudes they generated diffused into society as a whole and, as a matter of fact, can still be found among us.

Because of their widespread impact, and because their popularity gave them special dimensions and unique histories, they must be analyzed as part of a special category, which I have elected to label the "Grand Scene." I believe the label suggests that, in some period, among some large segment of the population, the hippie and surfing scenes were the dominant, most exciting, most appealing alternative lifestyles. This characteristic is the most important, but the most interesting and sociologically relevant facet of the surfing and hippie scenes is their histories. Both emerged and faded in a relatively short time, and both passed through very similar stages. This—and the fact that their evolution seems very like the process of ascendancy and decline experienced by social phenomena, such as social movements and fads— makes their histories particularly interesting. This chapter focuses primarily on the natural history of the surfing and hippie scenes.

Before turning to this natural history, however, we must more crisply distinguish this genre of scene. We have already mentioned three of its characteristics: (1) A large segment of the population perceived it as an appealing, prestigious lifestyle—as the "in" scene. (2) It involved at some point in its history hundreds of thousands of persons. (3) Its patterns extended from those directly involved to a much larger proportion of the population.

Two more characteristics fully distinguish this category, the first of which was also previously touched upon: (4) It is an alternative lifestyle. As defined earlier, the alternative lifestyle must involve a total or near total life-round—that is, a range of day and night activities—means of obtaining life's basics—shelter, clothes, and food—and a general belief and value system. In addition, to be an *alternative* lifestyle, it must involve essential activities which are unconventional, and a system of support consistent with the unconventional activities. The final distinguishing characteristic is that (5) it is relatively *open*. Insiders cannot exercise controls on who participates, nor can special or rare characteristics (such as extreme wealth) be conditions of membership.

THE NATURAL HISTORY OF THE GRAND SCENE

The Grand Scene, as seen from an analysis of its two exemplary types, passes through four distinct phases: (1) formation, (2) expansion (3) corruption, and (4) stagnation.

These phases correspond generally to those identified some years ago by L. S. Penrose in his analysis of "crazes." He suggested that crazes pass through (1) a "latent period (formation), during which the idea, though present in the minds of a few, shows little sign of spreading," (2) a phase "during which time the idea spreads rapidly" (expansion), (3) a period when "the susceptible minds becomes saturated," and in which there is a "development of mental resistance against the idea" (corruption). Finally, (4) the last phase (stagnation) is when the idea, if it "still persists, remains stagnant; either it is incorporated into the occasional habits of many or kept alive in the minds of a few enthusiasts."[1]

The similarity of these phases and those through which the Grand Scene passes supports the contention that this cycle is a general one. In addition to crazes or fads, which do not involve the complete life-round of traits that the Grand Scene does, other smaller scenes, such as the beatnik and folk music scenes of the late 1950s and early 1960s, followed a similar history. Social movements—collective activities aimed at producing basic social changes in the society, and typified by the 1960s radical, antiwar, and prison movements—also tend to follow this cycle. Consequently, the natural history of surfing and the hippies is not only fascinating in itself, but has, we believe, general relevance.

FORMATION

Several components are necessary for the occurrence of a lifestyle with sufficient refinement and excitement to attract hundreds of thousands of newcomers. First, there must be a group of people who share some interests and are engaged in collective activities related to those eventually adopted by the scene. These *core members* must be relatively free from other social activities. They must have contact with a large circle of *potential members* who are also relatively uninvolved in other social activities and who can therefore join in once the scene begins to take shape. Two overriding qualities characterize this period of articulation—the excitement mentioned above, and spontaneity. Among the core and potential members is a sense that something new, wonderful, and meaningful is happening, and they are part of it. Though at this stage—and this is very important—they can not fully describe or categorize their experiences, they constantly share their excitement, as well as their options on the various dimensions of the emerging scene. The *spontaneity* is manifest in that the scenes are being articulated by people relatively disaffiliated from other social-cultural forms. They are doing something original, unique, individual, "their own thing." This spontaneity is squashed in the next stages, but in the period of articulation it, along with the excitement, is the predominant mood of the scene articulators.

Surfers. Before World War II, there were about 500 surfers who lived on or close to the ocean in Southern California. They were, by and large, conventionally oriented middle-class young men who surfed for sport. About half of them were organized into seven or eight surfing clubs, whose activities not only included planning outings such as weekend excursions, but also, according to a couple of members of the oldest and best organized club, keeping other members from being drawn by surfing away from *serious* career plans.[2] World War II took these conventionally oriented young men away, and left behind at each beach town (i.e., Hermosa Beach, Manhattan Beach, Santa Monica, Venice, and Long Beach) a few teenage boys who had been hangers-on and patently were a different ilk. The best way to describe this class is to look at one surfer who was especially important to it—Dale Velzey. Velzey typifies the commitment and activities of the young men who inherited surfing because of World War II. In an earlier study of surfing, I wrote:

> Typical of these youths was Dale Velzey who began surfing at 12 years of age with the members of the Palos Verdes surf club. Dale, who had been left to his own pursuits more than most

youths, had been spending the majority of his time at the beach occupying himself with various activities such as digging sand crabs for spending money. Once he made contact with the surfers, who found this waif interesting, he became an ardent devotee to surfing. He tagged along with the older surfers whenever they would tolerate him. He spent more time at the beach than they because he refused to attend school beyond the eighth grade. While the other surfers were at work or in school he was at the beach, surfing or working on their surfboards. By the time he was eighteen he was already a veteran surfer, one of the most skilled in California. In addition to his skill in surfing, he had become one of the leading board craftsmen. When he was still in his early teens, because the price of a surfboard was far out of reach to him, he acquired a talent for patching up old boards. He nurtured this skill through the years and became one of the leading innovators and builders of surfboards. Later he became a leading surfboard manufacturer.

A surfer relates his impressions of Dale:

"He was the scraggliest, most unruly kid I had ever seen in my life. You just couldn't control this kid, but then you could never really get mad at him because he had something about him, some kind of spunk that made almost everyone like him. He used to get us mad by using our boards that we left down at the pier while we were working or at school. Sometimes he would bang them up, but he was good at repairing them and you just couldn't stay mad at Dale."

When the war began Dale was sixteen, and it was he and a few others of this age or younger who inherited surfing. At this time several of the youths went to work in the factories in Los Angeles and could afford automobiles, so Dale had transportation to start making surfing trips up and down the coast. In the last year of the war Dale went into the Merchant Marines, but returned in 1947 and again took up headquarters at the Manhattan pier. At this time he started spending more time making surfboards which he shaped under the Manhattan pier. Again, a small circle of surfers attached themselves to him. This group was typical of surfing groups after the war. They drank, loitered a great deal, and generally created an unusual picture with their peculiar beach dress (usually with bare feet, well-worn sailor pants often cut off short, and either with shirts, or possibly sporting flowered island shirts).

These were the core members necessary to generate a scene, supplied by the war, which also, incidentally, provided a larger number of potential members. Many returning veterans were not ready to resume a civilian life which, after the intensity of the war, seemed mundane or meaningless. Donald Becker, in a study of the postwar problems of veterans reported in *Social Forces* in 1946, quoted from a letter in which a veteran wrote of his difficulties in returning to civilian life.

> I have been feeling for the past six months a restlessness and intransigence that makes any job at all a burden. And it's not, curiously enough, because you don't want to work. On the contrary, I wish I could get buried in something that worked me night and day. In an indirect way I think we miss the over-riding purpose that was always present in, however attenuated, a form during the war—the purpose of winning the war. Now of course there ain't no purpose and the letdown will probably haunt us for some months to come. [p. 97].

The letdown was not unique to returning servicemen. A lot of Americans felt some degree of postwar disillusionment or depression which made them unwilling to return to conventional life. A postwar generation of disaffiliates emerged. Norman Mailer, in *Advertisements for Myself,* wrote about the "adventurers" who had been jarred off conventional tracks by the war or earlier events.

> That post war generation of adventurers who (some consciously, some by osmosis) had absorbed the lessons of disillusionment and disgust of the twenties, the depression, and the war, sharing a collective disbelief in the words of men who had too much money and controlled too many things, they knew almost as powerful disbelief in the coyly monolithic ideas of the single mate, the solid family and the respectable love life. [p. 292].

In addition to much of the postwar population being psychologically unwilling to return to the mundane routines of conventional life, they had the economic means to avoid doing so. The federal government's 52-20 (twenty dollars a week for fifty-two weeks for servicemen) was often extended by individual states, and the availability of unemployment compensation permitted an extended vacation. Consequently, beaches—as well as pool halls, bowling alleys, bars, and coffeehouses—experienced a rush of young people ready to participate in alternative lifestyles. In Los Angeles, surfing, like hot-rodding, motorcycling, and the drug life, had a supple of potential members. Dave Rochlen, who went into surfing after the war, described his feelings at the time in a 1964 issue of *Surf Guide*:

> When the war ended. . . .Boom, we were back in the enrivonment. It was devotion . . . like seeing a girl again . . . like I'm never gonna leave! Anyway, after the war we plunged into this thing . . . gave ourselves over to it entirely. I think it was because we had spent four or five years in the war and we had survived. And it had all been bad. Now there was no question about which had us by the throat. It was the ocean. Everything else was secondary [pp. 9-10].

The period of articulation of surfing lasted a relatively long time—at least five years (from 1947 to 1952). Actually we could stretch the period back into the war when Dale Velzey and Bob Simmons were vigorously experimenting with the patterns of surfing; and forward a few years because the experimentation, the excitement, and spontaneity were not completely killed until the late 1950s. Two reasons for the slowness of evolution was that the emerging surfing scene was out of sight of most urbanites, and since the mass media had not, as yet, revved up to full speed nor become as sensitive to "deviant" lifestyles as it was to become by the 1960s.

But 1947 to 1952 were the prime years for the core surfers creating the scene, most of whom centered themselves at Manhattan-Hermosa Beach, Malibu, or Windansea in La Jolla. A larger group, in addition to directly surfing, were generating the total surfing lifestyle with its dedication to the outdoors, the ocean, and to meeting the challenge of the waves without allowing any other intrusion. In terms of the enthusiasm and dedication it generated among the original surfers and the value of many of its inherent qualities, surfing in this period was every bit as exciting and fulfilling as the hippie scene, which has received much more attention. All things considered—the physical vigor, the thrills, the salubrity, and the uncomplicated, intense life focus—I'd choose it over any other period of recent history. Mickey Dora, a well-known surfer, hints at how good it was then by not wanting to talk about it now.

> The vintage years are over. I have my memories and that's it. I want to keep them to myself.

Hippies. There were two different categories of core members who eventually joined together to articulate the hippie scene—the old beats, and the folkniks. The more important of these came from older bohemians (over twenty-five), many of whom had been left over from the beatnik era (1955-1960). Several dozen of these bohemians lived in and circulated around different parts of the San Francisco Bay Area, but knew each other and crossed paths at several pockets or focal points, a few of which were in residences or coffeehouses around the University of California at Berkeley. After 1960, when beatniks spilled out of North Beach (the center of the beatnik scene) to the western part of San Francisco, pockets were found in "pads" near Haight-Ashbury—an ideal neighborhood because it was in transition and offered more space for less money than other areas of the city. In addition, there were some outlying pockets, such as Palo Alto's Perry Lane, a short street of low-rent cottages near Stanford University. Perry's Lane had become a bohemian center many years before and became one of the pre-hippie focal points when Ken Kesey moved there.

The beats were expanding into several new activities, which eventually led them to the hippie scene. The first of these was the use of a new class of drugs. For the most part, the beat scene ingested marijuana and wine, which fit its "cool" or pessimistic mood. By the end of the 1950s, however, after Aldous Huxley described in *Doors of Perception* his fantastic experiences on mescaline, many people began using peyote and its derivative, mescaline. Soon increasing amounts of peyote were carried or shipped to the Bay Area from the deserts of Arizona, New Mexico, and Mexico. After 1960, experimentation began with more sophisticated drugs in this same class, which were being synthesized by chemists. Tom Wolfe described (in *The Electric Kool-Aid Acid Test*) the impact of these drugs on Perry Lane.

> Volunteer Kesey gave himself over to science over at the Menlo Park Vets Hospital—and somehow drugs were getting up and walking out of there to Perry Lane, LSD, mescaline, IT-290, mostly. Being hip on Perry Lane now had an element nobody had ever dreamed about before, wild-flying, mind-blowing drugs. Some of the old Perry Lane luminaries' *cool* was tested and they were found wanting. [p. 41].

These drugs opened two other directions. The first was experimentation in new forms of art. Both in writing and in graphics, but particularly in the latter, the new drug experience pushed the beat artists into a search for more intense, abstract forms. Several people around the Bay Area were experimenting with light paintings—the projection of light through fluid, hand-manipulated paint pigments and dyes which cast a vivid swirling painting on a screen. Ken Kesey's book *One Flew Over the Cuckoo's Nest* showed the influence of this new artistic impulse, but his later venture into film-making was more directly an outcome of his drug experiences.

The second new direction was consciousness expansion. The new drugs seemed to open up unused areas of the mind and allowed hitherto unexperienced levels of awareness and consciousness. In fact, perceiving and savoring more of the world, and exploring the contours and corners of the mind, while high on the "psychedelic" drugs was probably the most significant activity of these pre-hippies.

The second group of core members in the hippie scene was made up of young San Francisco Bay Area folk musicians who had come along after the beat scene. They, like many other cadres of "folkniks" around the country, not only rejected conventional paths, but rejected rock and roll, the music of the screaming "teenyboppers," and jazz, the music of aging, white bohemian-intellectuals. In the late 1950s and early 1960s, these folk musicians, whose heroes were Huddie Ledbetter, Blind Lemon Jefferson, Woody Guthrie, and Pete Seeger, were looking for "authentic" American folk music. As soon as they learned to play instruments or could sing skillfully, they formed country music, blue grass, blues, or jug bands, and played and watched each other in several dozen coffeehouses and clubs in the Bay Area. Jerry Garcia, of the most important hippie band, the Grateful Dead, describes the contacts between these Bay Area musicians in the early 1960s.

> '61 or '62 I started playing coffee houses and the guys who were playing around then up in San Francisco at the Fox and Hounds, Nick Gravenites was around then, Nick the Greek they called him; Pete Stampfel from the Holy Modal Rounders, he was playing around there then. A real nice San Francisco guitar player named Tom Hobson that nobody knows about, he was one of these guys that was sort of lost in the folk shuffle, but he's still around and he's still great.
>
> Let's see . . . in Berkeley there was Jorma playing coffee houses about the same time that I was, and Janis. In fact, Jorma and Janis and I met at the same time. They played at the place in Palo Alto I played at a lot, called the Tangent. They came in one night and I just flipped out. Janis was fantastic, she sounded like old Bessie Smith records, and she was really good. And Paul Kantner was playing around: David Freiberg was playing around, David

and Micaela, they called themselves, him and his chick played left-handed guitar, they did these rowdy Israeli folk songs. Michael Cunney was around then too. He's a guy that's kind of like Pete Seeger's junior version, he's very good, still plays around, banjo and some. Let's see . . . a lot of the people that are around now, that are still doing stuff now.

Well, I wasn't really hanging out with them but our paths would be crossing, playing at the same place the same night and pretty soon after two or three years of running into them you're friends. You never planned it or anything like that, it's just what's happening [see Charles Reich and Jann Wenner, *Garcia: A Signpost to New Space*, 1972, p. 32].

The *potential members* for the hippie scene were the larger circle of Bay Area "outsiders" who had been involved in either the bohemian-intellectual-artist's life or the civil rights movement. More than likely, they alternatively or simultaneously participated in both, since these lifestyles overlapped considerably. As indicated above, the beatnik activities had wound down by 1960, and there were numbers of bohemian-oriented outsiders relatively uninvolved in other activities. The civil rights movement, the Berkeley Free Speech Movement, and then protests against the Vietnam war were building to a peak between 1964 and 1965. The activities in these interrelated movements had the effect of "radicalizing" or "deconventionalizing" large numbers of Bay Area residents, mostly young people or students who were free to participate in the major events of various protests, such as marches, demonstrations, and rallies. Because they were not fully immersed in the day-to-day organizational activities of the more radical individuals, however, they were ready to "drop out" when the hippie scene began to germinate. By 1965, the year the hippie scene was really articulated, sufficient troops of potential members stood ready to join in.

The difference in the length of the period of formation for the surfing and hippie scenes is dramatic. In surfing, the period stretched for at least five years. In the hippie scene, it lasted one short year. The greater visibility of the activities and the greater sensitivity of the media by 1965 were important factors. Also, the more fully developed theatrical mentality of the actors must be considered a factor. By the mid-sixties, life had become more like a theatre, particularly in the psychological orientation of the people who pieced together this scene. They were much more aware of, and oriented toward, alternative lifestyles—some were actually performers—and they were, therefore, more capable of "staging."

We will later examine at length the sequence of articulating events in which Ken Kesey was the central, but not the only, figure. Other people were similarly involved in San Francisco. Many of the heads and beats in San Francisco were beginning to mill around several common foci, LSD being one of the most important. There was a strong sense among the loose collectivity that something new was evolving and that they were a part of it.

The mixture of people and the time were right—the scene clicked. In fact, it achieved critical mass and, like a fission bomb, exploded and sent shock waves throughout the beat-hip levels of the city. A new age had clearly dawned, and now people could really groove together, free from their competitiveness, suspicions, individualism, and other "hang-ups."

BASIC ELEMENTS

In addition to members, in order for a scene to emerge there must be some elements out of which an refined and exciting lifestyle can be generated. Both surfing and the hippie scene had excellent basic material.

Surfing. The fundamental element of surfing, wave riding on a surfboard, was brought to Southern California as early as 1907, when a Hawaiian swimmer and surfer, George Freeth, traveled to the coast to introduce wave riding (the traditional sport of his royal ancestors) to the United States. Slowly the sport spread to a small number of middle- or upper-middle-class men (and a very few women) who lived near the beaches around Los Angeles and who had the strength to handle the eighty-pound Hawaiian-type surfboard.

These beginnings would be changed radically when later experimentation with the surfboard occurred, but the bare rudiments always remained the same. Wave riding entails getting a surfboard out into the ocean beyond the shore break, then paddling it toward shore. The wave catches up to the moving surfer just as it becomes steep enough to cause the board to slide on its face. The surfer must achieve a certain minimum paddling speed to start the sliding movement, and the wave must offer a steep enough surface to keep the board sliding, as if down a hill—but a hill which is constantly being reconstructed by the wave action. A wave travelling across the open ocean is not nearly steep enough to offer this type of slope; it only becomes sufficiently steep when it moves into shallow water. There the sea bottom interferes with the normal deep water wave action, which leads to the wave "breaking." A wave becomes steep enough for sliding on just before it breaks.

Before World War II, surfboards were made of redwood, the only wood light enough to result in a board that could "float" a person, be carried, and yet was strong enough to take the abuse the ocean gave it. (Balsa wood had been experimented with, but as soon as its outer coat of varnish was punctured, it soaked up water too fast to float for long.) This relatively heavy, cumbersome redwood board required a slowly breaking wave, which the coast of California offered at only a few locations, two of the best of which were the "Cove" on the Palos Verdes Peninsula and San Onofre, just south of San Clemente. Most of the coastline received waves which could not be ridden because they broke too fast.

But—because of wartime technology—all this changed during and after World War II. Fiberglass, a tough, light material which could be applied to any surface opened the way to experimentation with smaller, lighter boards which would float an individual and could take occasional knocks on hard surfaces. In addition, a board constructed from balsa was developed with a fin in the back to allow it to cross the slope of a wave diagonally instead of skipping down its face. Now anything could be ridden—larger waves, smaller waves, fast-breaking waves. Instead of having to go to the same surfing spots week after week, to ride the relatively flat waves which rolled gently to the shore at San Onofre and the Cove, the postwar surfers started searching for more and more difficult waves. When they found them, they rode them. Surfing had really become exciting. It involved taking off on steeper and bigger waves, traversing steep walls of water at high speeds, and executing turns in a manner which had previously been considered impossible.

The beach was the second basic element, which, fitted together with wave riding, built postwar surfing. In Southern California, the beach for decades has been a place where people can spend enjoyable days doing pleasant things. To many, it has been no more than a vacation or weekend spot where swimming, sunbathing, and volleyball can erase the strains and drudgery of routine urban worlds. But to others— and there have always been such others—it has represented a slower, less routinized, less aggravating, less frustrating, and less complicated way of life, a life closer to "nature," free of mechanization, responsibilities, commitments, or drudgery. Southern California beaches, like those of the South Seas, have long been a setting for the "beachcomber." Thus, the nonproductive, barefooted, beach-hobo tradition was prominent at the Southern California beaches and supplied some of the source material for the emerging surfing style.

Hippies. The people who pieced together the hippie scene had several basic elements available. Psychedelic drugs, as they were called by the "unofficial" experimenters, were the most important of them. As described earlier, the search for psychedelics became popular around 1960. *The Doors of Perception* had sensitized the hip crowd to the possibilities of these drugs. The medical and psychiatric professions were giving the drugs to various volunteers around the country, as well as in the Bay Area, and publishing narrow, misleading scientific reports regarding the drug experience.[3]

Finally, Timothy Leary, a psychologist from the University of California and then Harvard, began experimenting with the drugs. This, from the perspective of the august Harvard academic community, brought about bizarre experiments and his eventual termination from the university. Leary and Richard Alpert, his associate in these experiments, set up the Castalia Foundation in Mexico, began to publish a journal devoted to the psychedelic drug experience, and distributed LSD through informal networks.

Bay Area interest in the new drugs intensifed between 1961 and 1964. There was some peyote, but hardly any of the precious LSD. Volunteering for experiments and then smuggling some of the drugs away from the clinics did not satisfy the growing interest. Eventually, young Berkeley radical-bohemian chemists, particularly Owsley Stanley, learned the formula for LSD and started manufacturing it chemically on a large scale, which was not illegal in California until October of 1966. This made the new experience available to almost anyone who was interested and had contacts in the Bay Area bohemian circles.

Descriptions of the psychedelic drug experience have been widely varied and contradictory. In fact, the experience is so complex it defies translation into ordinary language (Tom Wolfe's description, in my opinion, is the best attempt). I'd like to avoid getting involved in the uncertain rhetoric, but an understanding of two recurring aspects of the experiences is necessarily relevant to the scene articulation. The first is the intense, sensory experience in which the world becomes an overwhelming, pulsating, vibrating mixture of sight, sound, and feeling. Motion and color are especially vivid. Paintings, flowers, still life pictures, scenery, and other inanimate objects come to life in undulating technicolor. Hands and other parts of the body seem visibly alive, the skin and hair moving and growing and the blood pulsing through the veins. Experimenting doctors speak of this sensory phenomenon as hallucinatory. The more mystical drug experimenters argue that the human is merely drawn closer to the essential living and moving reality of all things.

The second important aspect of the drug experience is the phenomenon of "de-categorization." While under the influence of the drug—particularly in the first few "trips"—one experiences the world as a mass of raw, unfamiliar data which must be classified. The taken-for-granted recipes, designs, standards, and definitions which categorize the world and oneself—though they can be recalled and actually applied under pressure—do not give the person a comfortable foundation for action. The interpretive categories can be called forth as if from a book being read by someone else and imparted as a guide through the strange psychedelic land. Each new event, however, is faced as if it had never been encountered before.

The reactions to this experience are, of course, as widely varied as the descriptions of it. Many people, particularly those who have not had a long initiation through marijuana use, panic. Others attempt simultaneously to make minimum sense out of the events they pass through and to savor the delicious sensory experiences.

A lingering effect of the experiences is that individuals continue to call into question their taken-for-granted frames of reference. Social facades and categories are shattered so thoroughly that they cannot be reconstructed for the next few days or even weeks. Of course, these frames of reference become even more permanently damaged by repeated trips. The destruction of basic, accepted beliefs usually results in an increased ability to reject old perspectives and understand alternate ones, and in a feeling of individual vulnerability and insignificance (which is often converted to a desire to establish community and interdependence with others).

In the same period that acid was being manufactured and distributed among the ex-beats, folk musicians, and other outsiders in the Bay Area, several strands of pop music were woven together to produce a new music, eminently suitable for this scene. One of these strands was the "authentic" American folk music mentioned earlier. For several years, people such as Bob Dylan had been recultivating the themes, moods, and styles of the great country and folk music heroes: Woody Guthrie, Blind Lemon Jefferson, Huddie Ledbetter, Pete Seeger, and others. The songs written and sung by these young folk musicians had modern themes like racial oppression, civil rights, and war. A second, related strand was the black "urban" blues which had developed through the thirties, forties, and fifties in Chicago, St. Louis, and Detroit. This music, with such old stars as Muddy Waters, Jimmy Reed, and B. B. King, had its own groups of young white devotees—young Negro blues imitators who joined in the mix. The last strand was the American "rock 'n' roll" of the Elvis Presley, Buddy Holly variety. The young American "folkniks" did not directly identify with this music, but it worked its way into the mixture by means of a circuitous route.

The initial mix which laid the way for the final synthesis of acid rock did not happen in America, but in England. English groups such as the Beatles and the Rolling Stones were, by 1963 and 1964, playing a combination of American rock and roll, Negro rhythm and blues, and Bob Dylan-type country-protest music. The English music was loud with a steady, hammering beat. In addition, the Beatles possessed an infectious exuberance and the Stones, a "funky" earthiness.

This music, particularly that of the Beatles, started attracting the attention of American teenagers in the last half of 1963. A fifteen-year-old East Coast teenager reports her reactions to the first time she hard the Beatles.

> I was going to the supermarket in the car with my mother one day, in our Jaguar, that's what we had at the time, though that's not important. Over the car radio came "I Want to Hold your Hand." It was the first time I'd heard of the Beatles. I went, "Wow! What a strange sound." I just couldn't get over it. No tune had ever affected me as much [Hunter Danes, *The Beatles,* 1969, p. 213].

Though at first confined to teenagers, Beatlemania swept from England to America. Then some talented English film-makers recognized the appealing vitality of the Beatles and built an artistic and entertainment masterpiece around them. "A Hard Day's Night" quickly became the "hip" movie of 1964, and older bohemians, hipsters, folkniks, and just plain people joined teenagers in seeing it once, twice, three times, or more. Besides being one of the best movies of the year, it raised the Beatles and their music from teenage noise and trivia to serious consideration as an English development of American music. The American folk scene did a radical turnabout overnight. Jerry Garcia explains why his jug band got into "electric stuff."

> Well Pigpen, as a matter of fact, it was Pigpen's idea. He'd been pestering me for awhile, he wanted me to start up an electric blues band. That was his trip . . . because in the jug band scene we used to do blues numbers like Jimmy Reed tunes and even played a couple of rock and roll tunes and it was just the next step.
>
> And the Beatles . . . and all of a sudden there were the Beatles, and that, wow, the Beatles, you know. "Hard Day's Night," the movie, and everything. Hey, great, that really looks like fun [Garcia, p. 377].

All over the Bay Area, country folk musicians laid down their acoustical guitars and started playing "electric stuff." Even Dylan, the hero of the purists, cut a single called "Like a Rolling Stone," with a fully electrified, loud, rock sound. In his 1965 tour, with the Paul Butterfield Blues Band, made up of the Chicago Blues imitators, he was ill-received by audiences. In *Rock Revolution,* Richard Robinson described Dylan's 1965 tour.

> His concerts were now half-acoustic, half-electric and the fans were split the same way. At the Newport Folk Festival (1965), where he was backed up by the Paul Butterfield Blues Band (which featured Michael Bloomfield and Al Kooper) he was nearly hooted out of town [p. 51].

Like the psychedelic experience, the new rock music was too complex and too variegated to permit a simple, short characterization. For our purposes, it is enough to agree that most of the music involved amplified guitars, organs, and other such instruments, and a background of loud steady drumming. Lyrics were often more poetically and ideologically serious than rock and roll had been, but the music's principal quality was its acoustical intensity.

In addition to the two basic elements—psychedelics and acid rock—there were at least two other components which fit into the articulation. One was the intense new art forms, mentioned earlier. The older beats, influenced greatly by peyote and LSD, were experimenting with freer, bolder uses of color and other material. The light shows and the colorful posters which were integral parts of the emerging hippie scene were prime examples of their artistic innovations. The second component, again followed by old beats in new moods, was unusual clothes. In 1962, 1963, and 1964, full-length velvet dresses, cowboy outfits, high button shoes, old men's suits, and other old and unusual things, such as Benjamin Franklin glasses, all made their appearance from closets, attics, and junk shops on McAllister Street in San Francisco. By 1964, on Haight Street and at parties around town, the pre-hippies were turning out in what was, for those years, very strange attire.

TERRITORIES

In addition to members and elements, an emerging scene which will achieve the heights required to be *the* scene must possess a specific territory or territories. [4] There must be some place or places where the members of the emerging scene can find each other in order to get together on a regular basis and engage in face-to-face activities related to the elements of the scene, and it must be a location where they have territorial rights and cannot be displaced. Moreover, once the scene begins to take hold, locations are necessary so that people who want to plug into the activities can find them.

With our modern communication systems, it is possible for a great deal of articulation to occur in "space," but even with the speed and pervasiveness of modern media, a considerable amount of face-to-face interaction, discussion, informal and formal planning must occur if a new perspective and a new set of cohesive life patterns are to be developed. When this sort of direct contact does not occur, as will be seen later, a scene quickly loses its original forms and meanings, and is corrupted.

Surfing. Surfing had several territories which were controlled by the postwar surfers. Most of these were on the ocean, usually at preferred surfing spots. Two locations stand out— Manhattan Pier, where Dale Velzey made surfboards and met with his cohorts, and "Malibu," a surfing spot just north of the Malibu Pier. At these locations, particularly in the summer, some surfers could be found on the beach or in the water at any time of the day, whether or not there were waves to ride.

In addition to the locations on the beach, there were garages and small shops in the beach towns in which surfboard craftsmen built and repaired boards. When the weather was bad, there was no surf, or it was dark, the core surfers were able to locate each other and spend time together in these alternate territories.

Hippies. There were at least two primary territories for the articulation of the hippie scene, the first of which was the

Haight-Ashbury district of San Francisco. By 1965, the "Haight" was becoming the new Greenwich Village. It was a perfect neighborhood for bohemians, in that it was changing from a heterogeneous working-class white area to a primarily black district. The rents were dropping, there was a surplus of apartments in the handsome wood Victorian houses which characterized old San Francisco, and it was close to Golden Gate Park. There was good transportation to other parts of the city, and Haight Street was one of the more interesting, older shopping districts. When the scene started to take shape in 1964-1965, there was an increase in the influx of hippies and for a year the "straight" community—particularly the merchants—attempted to stop the invasion. However, the hippies and pre-hippies who had started opening coffee-houses, dress shops, and psychedelic stores, and who consti-tuted a "hip merchant" class, organized and succeeded in thoroughly opening the area for hippies.

Haight Street kept evolving for the next couple of years. There was already a leftover beatnik-type coffee shop, the Blue Unicorn, and in 1965, a bohemian-type dress shop and a coffeehouse opened. In January 1966, the Psychedelic Shop opened. It sold records, incense, roach clips, posters, and other exotic "head" accoutrements. The street was well on its way. When the new age dawned, it was generally recog-nized that its center was the Haight-Ashbury, and the influx into the neighborhood accelerated accordingly.

A second important territory was Ken Kesey's ranch in La Honda. This spot was reserved for the core members, who knew Kesey, knew people who knew Kesey, or knew people who had made the trek down to the ranch before. Included in this crowd were some of the early key figures of the hippie scene, such as Neil Cassady and Ralph Ginsberg. The ranch, where the whole forest seemed to be wired for sound and painted in DayGlo, provided the location for some of the most intense articulation of the hippie scene.

There were other territories, such as Telegraph Avenue

in Berkeley, which were partly dominated by the pre- and early hippies. However, the University of California continued to generate activities, such as the war protests, which competed with the hippie scene. Finally, there were a few additional, outlying spots similar to the Kesey ranch—such as Muir Beach in Marin County north of San Francisco—where early hippies rented old cabins and houses, and musicians and other core members flowed in and out.

In addition, Longshoreman's Hall in San Francisco was the site of a series of dances begun in late 1965 by several "core" people who had been associated with a saloon in Nevada and called themselves "The Family Dog." The dances—with names like "A Tribute to Dr. Strangelove," "A Tribute to Sparkle Plenty," or "A Tribute to Ming the Merciless"—featured the new rock groups (The Jefferson Airplane, Great Society, The Mothers, The Lovin' Spoonful), a lot of people in weird costumes, and acid. Bill Graham, a member of the San Francisco Mime Troop, a radical, "guerilla" theatre group which had been hassling with the city administration and the police, put on three benefits after the Mime Troop was arrested for staging an unauthorized performance in the Panhandle of the Golden Gate Park (which runs through the Haight-Ashbury district). Later Ken Kesey came to town with what he called his "acid tests," and then presented a weekend "Trips Festival" at the Hall. Finally, Bill Graham leased the Fillmore Auditorium and started a long series of dances, and Chet Helm, using the name "The Family Dog," leased the Avalon Ballroom and presented his own weekly dances. But these were all anti-climaxes, for a whole scene burst into full, beautiful flower at the first two or three dances in Longshoreman's Hall, put on by the original Family Dog members—Luria Castell, Jack Towle, Ellen Harmon, and Alton Kelly.

CHARISMATIC LEADERS

In addition to its basic elements, the Grand Scene needs charismatic leaders to lead to its full articulation. In its initial stage, an elegant and appealing lifestyle must involve highly creative persons, and leaders to give the new forms legitimacy. During a scene's period of formation, most people are probing in new social and cultural directions, which can produce anxiety and insecurity among the less secure or courageous. Charismatic leaders can give these hesitant followers confidence and stability. In addition, charismatic leaders serve as personifications of the new style. This is the general function of folk heroes—their lives give reality to some ideal form which others are pursuing. So it is with the scene.

The hippie and surfing scenes had their charismatic leaders: Dale Velzey, Dewey Weber, and Phil Edwards for surfing; Chet Helms, Neil Cassady, and Emmet Grogan for the hippies. However, in each scene there is one standout individual, who was involved in the early stages when the most adventurous explorations occurred and when articulation was in its major growth period. The two men are Bob Simmons and Ken Kesey. (Interestingly, neither was still involved when the two scenes peaked).

Bob Simmons. Bob Simmons was one of the young "unconventional" youths who inherited surfing at the beginning of War War II. He had started surfing just before the war, when he was about twenty. At this age, Simmons was very thin and had a crippled arm as a result of an earlier bicycle accident. A surfer once told me that when he first saw Simmons, soon after Simmons had started surfing, he found it incredible that Simmons could ever hope to master the sport. With fantastic tenacity, he did and became in fact one of the most highly skilled surfers in the early days of the scene.

Simmons was unusual in many ways. His disposition was extreme. He was morose, unfriendly, irritable, and argumentative, and nobody—not even those who associated with him over a period of time—felt particularly close to him. But everyone who surfed in the years 1945-1955 knew of his exploits, ideas, and contributions, since these had such a profound impact on surfing.

> He had a better mind than any of us guys. He was a man. He neither gave nor asked quarter from anyone. "_____all you guys." He was a loner . . . beautiful. He lived in Pasadena. He had his red blazer and travelled up and down the coast towing that piece of redwood on his stupid wagon. I say here's why he was a man: he didn't need to see somebody else doing something . . . didn't need somebody else to jazz him. He had it right inside him [Rochlen, p. 10].

He either created or firmly established most of the trends which became basic patterns of surfing and he was constantly searching for and trying to ride waves at new surfing spots. He opened one impossible or unknown location after another. He was one of the first California surfers to go to Hawaii after World War II, looking for bigger waves. Simmons was the first to attempt Sunset Beach, which had not been ridden by Hawaiians for decades and which is now considered one of the most exciting surfing spots in the world. Because of his impaired swimming ability and the strong rip tides there, he could only make the attempt with someone standing by in a rowboat. But he rode the spot—as well as many other places which had not been ridden before he conquered them.

His innovations in the boards themselves were even more important to surfing. He had had some experience in woodworking before he took up surfing, and he applied these skills and his natural intelligence to board design. After a great deal of experimentation (in which he was not the only participant), he developed a board constructed from balsa wood covered with fiberglass, which was much smaller and lighter than the redwood boards, with a fin in back to keep it traversing the wave. Most surfers considered this board too unstable and slow, but Simmons proved both notions false. He kept perfecting and vehemently defending the board in many informal discussions among the core surfers of those years. The board he designed revolutionized surfing and became the prototype for the modern surfboard.

Simmons was killed while surfing at Windansea, La Jolla, in 1954. Surfers have told many versions of the death in later years. Chris Keifer was a contemporary of Simmons' who heard about the death immediately after it occurred:

> The surf that day was the biggest it had been in three or four years. Del Mar was unsurfable in the morning, being walled up and crashing straight over. Some sets were over fifteen feet, I think. In the afternoon several "regulars" from the Windansea came up, and described the scene down there. One guy said there were twenty or more surfers 'out' all day—very unusual in these days—and a great deal of confusion. Everybody was keeping an eye on Simmons because of his handicap. Several people told me that the shoreline was littered with bits of balsa and fiber glass from the boards that had been demolished by the famous Windansea shore break. (I saw this myself the following day.) The first anybody missed Simmons was when his board washed up without him. One of the beach boys got it and paddled it out to give it to him—the custom with Simmons, since he couldn't swim worth a damn. He couldn't find Simmons. A search was organized and several of the better surfers risked their necks paddling into dangerous areas looking for him. There was a strong rip running and a couple of guys paddled out to the kelp beds to look. It got too dark, finally, to keep looking. I was told a couple days later that he was found floating in the kelp beds the next day.

Ken Kesey.[5] Ken Kesey, as related earlier, was one of the first pre-hippie drug seekers who volunteered for the mèdical experiments with LSD and other synthesized hallucinogenics. At that time, he was attending Stanford on a creative writing fellowship and living on Perry Lane in Palo Alto. Kesey's hickish charm and Western swagger had captivated the Lane, which was an established intellectual-bohemian community Thorstein Veblen had lived there, and published writers were living along the Lane when Kesey moved in. Then Kesey started smuggling drugs out of the Menlo Park Clinic (along with peyote from Arizona). His probing deeper and farther out into the literary and human interactional netherlands soon became too much for many of the Lane's more respectable intellectuals, but others, more adventurous, joined him on these excursions into hitherto unexplored territories.

After his plunge into psychedelics, Kesey stopped the book he'd been working on and wrote *One Flew Over the Cuckoo's Nest*—sometimes writing while high on peyote. When it was finished, he left for Oregon for a few months and immersed himself in the logger's world to prepare for another book. By the time he got back to the Lane, *Cuckoo's Nest* had been published to rave reviews, and word of Kesey's drug exploits had reached many of the advance guard for the Bay Area heads and hipsters. They descended on the Lane to be around Kesey. Neil Cassady, of Jack Kerouac's *On the Road*, Richard Alpert, one of the original psychedelic proselytizers, and other notables of the beat, hip, drug world were among them.

Perry Lane was purchased by developers, and Kesey and his family moved to the ranch in La Honda, a beautiful, relatively undeveloped, mountainous spot forty miles south of San Francisco. There he continued to host the old Perry Lane crowd and newcomers from the Bay Area, who wanted to go in the directions which Kesey, more than any other person, was pointing out. By the time he finished his second novel, *Sometimes a Great Notion,* the multifaceted new scene was starting to come together, right there on his ranch in La Honda. There were the new psychedelic art forms. The trees were painted in DayGlo, sported strange mobiles from their limbs, and carried speakers, which were also on top of the house. Music was everywhere, giving background to the trips through the doors of perception opened by LSD and other psychedelics. There were the regular group sessions which Tom Wolfe labeled "marathon encounters in group therapy" for the young and "unfucked up," in which Kesey led the regulars, many of whom had established permanent residence on the grounds, down through the layers of the self and human relations.

After his second novel was done and money from the first was pouring in, Kesey directed his intense creativity in an even more psychedelic direction. He bought a bus and thousands of dollars' worth of filmmaking equipment, and with a group of close devotees, who had assumed the name of the Merry Pranksters, took off on a tour of the country. The bus was appropriately decorated in DayGlo and fully wired for sound. Riders could talk to each other from any part of the bus, or over loudspeakers to people on the street. They left for the New York World's Fair, wearing crazy costumes, taking plenty of acid. After the tour, including a visit with Timothy Leary at his New York institute (a mistake, because the Pranksters and the "True Believer" mystics didn't mix, even if they both used acid) and several thousand feet of film (most of it out of focus), they came back to La Honda.

When they returned, the scene was speeding up in the Bay Area. More and more acid was circulating and the Beatles' "A Hard Day's Night" had converted the folk music world. Kesey and his Pranksters began to search for ways to involve larger groups in multisensory, mind-blowing experiences. They had pulled off several grand "trips" at the ranch, one a weekend party for the San Francisco Hell's Angels in which the acid, music, and good vibes swirled through the forest, and even the usually belligerent Hell's Angels conducted themselves in something passing for a peaceful, loving manner. By this time, Jerry Garcia, a peninsula youth who had been playing guitar for years and had recently accumulated around him first a jug band and then, after "A Hard Day's Night," a rock band, had been coming to the ranch fairly regularly. Kesey and his followers decided to stage a large get-together in some urban setting which would attract and involve more people in the things the Pranksters had developed on the ranch and the bus trip: acid, color, slides, the Dead's music, and the mind-exploding spontaneous outgushing of human feeling. The first and second "acid tests," as they were called, were held in private homes in Santa Cruz and San Jose. Then there was a series of acid tests in Palo Alto, Muir Beach, Portland, and finally San Francisco, including one at the Fillmore Auditorium. These led to the more famous weekend "Trips Festival" at Longshoreman's Hall and to the long series of dances at the Fillmore, the Avalon, Fillmore East, and Winterland. But the first series of acid tests was the most important crucible of the hippie scene. Tom Wolfe, in his book on Kesey, argues that the whole scene began with these events.

> Even details like psychedelic poster art, the quasi-*art nouveau* swirls of lettering, design and vibrating colors, electro-pastels and spectral DayGlo, came out of the Acid Prankster styles with a sophistication the Pranksters never dreamed of. *Art is not eternal, boys.* The posters became works of art in the accepted cultural tradition. Others would even play the Dead's sound more successfully, commercially, anyway, then the Dead. Others would do the mixed-media thing until it was pure ambrosial candy for the brain with creamy filling every time. To which Kesey would say: "They know *where* it is, but they don't know *what* it is" [p. 224].

I think Tom Wolfe has simplified the development too much in this passage, and given too much exclusive credit to the Pranksters and the tests because at the same time other people were staging crucial events in San Francisco. (We will discuss these in the section to follow.) However, the activities of the Pranksters were certainly as important as those of anyone else, and it was Kesey's brilliance, confidence, and originality that led to new realms of experience.

At the time of the Trips Festival (January 1966), Kesey's legal difficulties mounted. He had been arrested for possession of marijuana in April of 1965, and received a six month's suspended sentence. However, he was arrested again two nights before the Trips Festival and after being released on bail, he fled to Mexico, where he stayed for nine months. Again, he was arrested and released on bail. He remained in the Bay Area until he was sentenced to six months in jail. Before he began his sentence, he unsuccessfully tried to steer the rapidly expanding hippie scene away from drugs, by holding a "graduation" ceremony. It is impossible to discern whether he was sincere in this gesture or was simply attempting to soften up the judge and prosecutor before his upcoming sentencing. It was clear that Kesey had left the scene or the scene had left Kesey. Nevertheless, he had shaped it more than had anyone else, and without his leadership or that of persons like him, scenes like the hippie scene or surfing cannot take shape.

THE GOLDEN AGE OF SURFING

Sometime around 1950 the various parts of the surfing scene had coalesced into an identifiable, full-time, alternative lifestyle. There followed a period during which the scene was at its peak in terms of refinement and cohesion. In fact, this very refinement and cohesion set into motion the processes of the scene's destruction. Before turning to these later stages, however, we must describe the major patterns and meanings of the surfing scene at its best.

WAVE RIDING

As you would expect, many basic meanings and patterns of vintage surfing surrounded riding the wave. I see these as breaking into three clusters. The first involves surfing as a challenge, which mainly entails finding bigger and more difficult waves and new surfing spots. The hunt began in California, but soon after the war it moved to Hawaii. A few small groups of surfers rediscovered that waves on the North Shore of Oahu, in the winter, reach thirty feet. Contemporary Hawaiian surfers had considered these waves unsurfable, and tended to restrict their surfing to the gentle waves at Wakiki. But now growing numbers of California explorers attempted and successfully rode one "impossible" location after another. The Hawaiians themselves quickly joined in this search for challenges and began surfing the "North Shore."

The second cluster of meanings is related to "making the wave." The basic procedures are catching the wave, turning the board away from the breaking portion and staying in front of the "white water" until the wave "flattens out" or starts to break, and the surfer "kicks out," "rides out the top," or "turns down." What this means is that a cycle has been completed, and the surfer has ridden the best sections of the wave without losing his surfboard. Making the wave can be very difficult, especially if the wave is fast-breaking and breaks in long sections ("closes out"), a condition which doesn't give the surfer much time to cross its face and get out. When a surfer gets a "hot takeoff," makes "the tube"—which is a steep section of the wave curling over and completely enveloping the surfer—and gets back out of the wave, he feels pure ecstasy.

> It's like . . . you take the toughest nut in the world and you crack it so it comes out whole. This takes preparation and know-how and skill—like the diamond cutter. And that's what you do when you get in the right place and make the right move [Rochlen, p. 11].

The third cluster of meanings and patterns related to wave riding is "going surfing." Going surfing, besides plenty of wave riding, could mean hours passed on a remote, secluded beach away from the "ugliness" of civilized life—being around a fire after coming half-frozen out of the winter waters, and talking over waves made and not made. The ocean itself was part of this cluster. It was more than just the locus of waves; the waves themselves were merely manifestations of something more profound. The ocean represented a primeval way of life and a force that was the antithesis of the mechanized, routinized, tame civilization that ended physically and philosophically at its boundaries.

The elaborate rendition of going surfing was the surfing "safari"—a planned surfing trip which lasted several days or longer. It may have been a short trip of a hundred miles or less down the coast to Trestles (a surfing spot near a railroad trestle south of San Clemente) or a trip to the islands lasting several weeks or months. The surfing safari fulfilled a very special function in the development of the patterns and meanings of surfing. Values, beliefs, and symbolic systems that emerge in a scene do so out of the participants' interaction in common activities. In the surfing scene, this process reached its optimum intensity in the surfing safari, in which there were a complex of things that were "surfing"—camping at some remote beach, daily surfing a maximum of hours, cooking and eating meals at the beach, spending the hours while not surfing watching and discussing surfing. These were everything surfing meant, condensed into a limited time and space.

THE BOARD

The drive to meet the challenge and make harder and harder waves also propelled surfers in an ancillary direction—i.e., the search for a better board. As mentioned earlier, several core members of the scene were deeply involved in this activity, even before the scene was fully articulated. They were searching for a board which would turn faster and would "hang" into a steeper wave—that is, would cross a steep wave diagonally without skipping down its face. The modern surfboard emerged directly as a result of these efforts. It was first made of balsa, then polyurethane foam, and covered with fiberglass and synthetic resin. It was much lighter (20-35 pounds) than the older redwood boards (80+ pounds), smaller, and had a deep tail fin (skeg) to keep the board traveling in a straight line. There are still many variations on this board design, but all have the basic qualities of relative lightness, smaller size, and a skeg.

In addition to the experimenting with board designs,

securing a board, keeping it in repair and transporting it were all activities which demanded some of the surfer's time and made alterations in their life routines. Until the middle fifties, when the surfboard industry began to gear up, securing a board was difficult, since they were all made in small workshops by individual craftsmen. Transporting the board also posed problems. Some cars, especially small ones, had to be modified specifically to carry the surfboards.

Finally, the board was a very important symbol to surfers. It was an object of beauty which they decorated in a variety of ways. More importantly, it was the cherished symbol of their central activity, to which they were devoted and which they often displayed quite proudly.

THE BEACH

Before, after, or between wave riding, the surfers spent many hours together on the beach, sitting perhaps in the sun or around a fire to warm up after the chilly water. During these periods, they talked, usually about surfing. If a group contained some strangers, information was exchanged about each other's experiences, different surfing spots, and different surfers. If others were still in the water, the group on the beach could watch and talk about the rides.

On days when there was no surf, the surfers could still spend many hours on the beach waiting for surf.

> We used to sit down there at Malibu just looking at each other and asking when the surf was going to come up. We'd even call up Hap Jacobs and ask when the surf was going to come up—he was supposed to know because he made surfboards [Rochlen, p. 12].

On some occasions the nonsurfing beach activities were more festive. Wine, beer, and food would be obtained by taking up a collection or would be donated by some generous (and solvent) surfer. There were usually guitar or ukulele players present and the group would gather together and sing, eat, and drink. These impromptu festivities could often go on for hours, especially if the group grew large.

In addition to surfing and spending a lot of daytime on the beach, surfers very often slept there, especially when on a surfing expedition. The most common method of sleeping at the beach was in a car; the station wagon and the panel or pickup truck were especially suited for this function. Sometimes cars which had been converted to board carriers had also been modified to afford a flat area where a mattress could be thrown. Many surfers spent long periods, often the entire summer, at one of the various surfing locations in this fashion.

The beach contributed to the surfers' clothes and styles of grooming. Their dress has always been one or another variation on traditional beach clothing. After the war, light or dark blue sailor pants were popular, worn with bare feet and a T-shirt, no shirt at all, or a Hawaiian flower shirt. Later, Bermuda shorts or blue Levis and T-shirts, but no shoes, became stylish. After 1955, huarache sandals, tennis shoes, and "Mazatlans" (Mexican sandals with soles made from old automobile tires) became preferred footwear. Hair was long and left to hang down uncombed on the sides. The surfer greatly—and deliberately—resembled a beachcomber.

Finally, the Southern California beaches, with their benign climate for so much of the year, made this lifestyle economically feasible, since they reduced or eliminated most ordinary life expenses. In the summer, clothing and housing costs could be almost completely eliminated. Food and the upkeep of a surfboard were the only unavoidable expenses, and they were often met by savings from former periods of employment, unemployment benefits, part-time work (often in the sorfboard industry), or dependence on friends and family.

COMEDY

A special type of comedy became quite prominent in the golden age of surfing. Its major manifestation was in the "character," who had the qualities of a jester or buffoon. The

following example occurred at a popular surfing hangout in
Hermosa Beach.

> I remember one Easter Sunday afternoon I was sitting at 22nd
> Street in Hermosa and all of a sudden I heard this congo drum,
> with somebody screaming "Has the Lord God come to thee?" I
> looked over the wall and there was Mike Zutell with an eight foot
> cross and he had his yellow terrycloth bathrobe, he had this beard
> that looked like the real thing. He had a pair of shades on and a
> beret and sandals and was carrying a bottle of Thunderbird and
> he had a loaf of bread in his pocket. He walked down the Strand
> and stopped at 22nd Street, and he served Communion to us all.
> People on the beach couldn't believe it [Henry Ford, p. 16].

A San Diego surfer told me another revealing incident.

> A group of Windansea surfers in about 1953 got Nazi costumes
> somewhere (SS uniforms with boots, hats, insignias, etc.) and
> attracted attention to themselves by directing traffic in down-
> town La Jolla. Following this incident, Nazi salutes, swastikas,
> and phoney German accents enjoyed a brief popularity through-
> out the San Diego county surfing community.

Nazi traits were to reappear in surfing with a slightly different emphasis, and we will discuss this in the next chapter. At
this time, the Nazi impersonation was done for its humor.
There were no political or ideological considerations in this
or later eruptions of Nazi styles. Surfers emphasized and
enjoyed such styles simply because of the fantastic and
incongruous spectacle they presented when contrasted with
lifestyles in the larger society. In general, the surfing "character" chose to make a spectacle of himself in conventional
eyes, while pointedly remaining unabashed. He was not performing for the conventional society (it was not even necessary for outsiders to see the acts, though it was more
convincing when they did), but for his own reference
group who were amused by his act. At least part of their
pleasure came from seeing someone being ridiculous by
conventional standards of propriety without caring, and

thereby vicariously enjoying a complete release from conventional norms.

HIPPIES AT THEIR PEAK

THE NEW PHILOSOPHY

Hippies were much more philosophical than surfers. Consequently, they developed a highly sophisticated and relatively explicit ethic which was an essential component of their lifestyle, particularly in the peak years. J. L. Simmons and Barry Winograd, two sociologists who were studying the emerging youth movement in 1964, just before the scene's full articulation, supply us with a good analysis of what they called the "hang loose" ethic. First, it was characterized by irreverence.

> It repudiates, or at least questions, such cornerstones of conventional society as Christianity, "my country, right or wrong," the sanctity of marriage and premarital chastity, civil obedience, the accumulation of wealth, the right and even competence of parents, the schools, and the government to head and make decisions for everyone—in sum, the Establishment [It's Happening, 1966, p. 12].

Second, it was infused with a basic humanism, a belief in the worth and potential of all people.

> Adherents don't necessarily proclaim the rationality of men or their inherent "goodness," but they do claim that people are precious and that their full development is perhaps the most worthwhile of all things [p. 13].

It emphasized the basic, unquestionable goodness of human experience. "The idea is that a great variety and depth of experience is beneficial and not at all harmful as long as you can handle it" (p. 14).

Spontaneity, as well, was well-regarded. "We find that spontaneity, the ability to groove with whatever is currently happening, is a highly valued personal trait" (p. 15). Finally, the ethic defended a general tolerance for other people and their activities. "Do whatever you want to as long as you don't step on other people while doing it" (p. 15).

Many of the major hippie patterns—the ridicule of "middle-class" values and behavior, the free, uninvolved sexuality, the spontaneous public outbursts of unconventional and sometimes illegal behavior, and the avid, often obnoxious defense of doing your own thing—sprang directly from this ethic, which the early flower children tried tenaciously to live by.

THE TRIP

If the ethic was a cornerstone of the hippie scene, the "trip" was the ground on which it rested. It was the trip, after all, which gave rise to the new perspective and the new ethic. The prototypal trip is the LSD (or other psychedelic drug) experience. We have dealt with this phenomenon before, stressing two of its aspects: enhanced sensory experiences and decategorization. These profoundly influenced the hippie ethic. Moreover, there was a general belief that the acid trip, the most important occurrence in the hippie scene, must be periodically experienced by all truly hip and liberated people.

Besides the drug trip, the related experience of "tripping out" in one's day-to-day activities was an essential aspect of the hippie life. Tripping out was the deep appreciation of ordinary things and events: a leaf, a rock, a "Star Trek" episode, or a short walk on the beach. It was this part of the hippie experience which was expressed in the most commonly used terms and phrases: "wow," "far out," "too much," and "that was really a trip!"

THE HAPPENING

In a world of individual trips, special, occasional, collective trips—happenings—put the icing on the hippie life. A happening, according to Sherri Cavan, in *The Hippies of the Haight,* involved multiple activities.

> When there is, in some specifiable area simultaneously music *and* dancing, *and* talking *and* admiring *and* singing *and* being, there is a happening [p. 101].

I would add that for an occasion of multiple activities to achieve happening status, a flow of *spontaneous* activity had to be generated. This was difficult to achieve. First, there had to be a tacit agreement among those present that vigorous, open expression was appropriate and would not be negatively sanctioned. Usually, this required a few uninhibited, relatively confident, respected leaders to begin the vigorous activities. Otherwise the multiple activities might constitute just another boring event, instead of a happening.

There were lots of minor happenings in the hippie scene, and several major ones. One of the best was staged by the Hell's Angels and the Diggers—a prominent group in the hippie scene.

> The Frisco Angels wanted to repay the people of the Haight for having come through with their brothers' bail. The club wanted to throw a party and Angel Pete talked about it with Emmett. They decided to have one in the Panhandle on New Year's Day and they did. It was called the New Year's Day Wail! And the Angels bought beer, which they gave away to everyone, and paid for the PA system. Emmett arranged for an eighteen-foot flatbed truck to be used as a stage. Since it was early Sunday afternoon, Emmett had to go wake up Big Brother and the Holding Company, as well as the Grateful Dead. Pearl cursed his being to infinite damnation, and Jerry Garcia suggested he go play Russian Roulette with a loaded automatic, but they came and he played his beautiful guitar licks and she sang her trashy soul out for the people.

> It was a great day and a hell of a party—the first free rock-concert-party in any city park put on solely by the people for themselves. By late afternoon everybody was high and happy. The cops came, saw the way everyone looked wasted, and split,

muttering something about the absence of a park permit. The crowd shouted a goodby after them: *"The parks belong to the people! The parks belong to the people"* [Emmett Grogan, *Ringolevio,* p. 301].

SHARING

The final major component of the hippie scene which we shall describe is sharing. To fully understand this dimension, one must remember that this took place before the energy crisis, when the general belief in the permanent material opulence of the American society was still strong. In fact, when the flower children grew up, the concept of "hard times" had been left far behind. For years there had been serious discussion of the problems which surrounded excess production and the forced leisure of those poor unfortunates who had to be dropped from their jobs because of the super-productive, automated industrial world. The hippies had an easy and philosophically consistent solution to these problems—drop out of the work force and share all material objects.

In the first year or two, they did share with one another. There were many communes in the Haight, loosely organized so it was not hard for people to find a place to live and a group with whom to share. Many of these had such a flow of rootless hippies that they were called "crash pads." Money and commodities were also shared. In the beginning, there were sufficient money and commodities *to* share because many of the hippies had savings, unemployment benefits, or college allowances from home. In addition, a growing number of commercial enterprises in the Haight used hippie labor. They did not pay well, but the hippies did not need much money. When the hippie newspapers started, anyone could pick up some change selling them on the street, in the Haight as well as in other parts of the city. Finally, the sharing philosophy was easily applied to panhandling, which the hippies did in all parts of San Francisco.

This perspective on material—that all material should be freely shared—had its most organized manifestation in the free food and other free commodities programs of the Diggers. This loosely organized group of people managed to maintain a store in which all goods were donated and given away free, and for several months served a daily free meal in the Panhandle. They even constructed an ideology of sharing that several Diggers pushed as the solution to the problems of a capitalist society. One of the Diggers wrote:

> The Diggers are hip to property. Everything is free, do your own thing. Human beings are the means of exchange. Food, machines, clothing, materials, shelter and props are simply there. Stuff. A perfect dispenser would be an open Automat on the street. Locks are time consuming. Combinations are locks.
>
> So a store of goods or clinic or restaurant that is free becomes a social art form. Ticketless theater. Out of money and control [Grogan, p. 345].

The patterns of sharing, like the patterns surrounding beach life in the surfing scene, made the hippie scene a viable, full-time nonproductive lifestyle—at least in its initial stage. Obviously, there were inherent flaws in this economic foundation. What is possible for a few thousand is not possible for several hundred thousand. There were, of course, similar flaws in the surfing scene. When they both continued to expand, these flaws grew into defects which would destroy the scenes' original beauty. We will look in the next chapter at the demise of the Grand Scene.

4 | The DEMISE of the GRAND SCENE

Neither the hippie scene nor surfing had control over its membership. Each drew more people than it could absorb and still maintain its original form. Consequently, both expanded too rapidly, stretched into grotesque shapes, and became unrecognizable and no longer appealing. The sequence which began with formation continued with expansion, then corruption, and finally stagnation. We will examine these stages below, because, as indicated earlier, we believe them to be generally applicable to all scenes.

EXPANSION

As a matter of fact, the expansion of the surfing and hippie scenes began while they were still taking shape. Before and during formation, growing numbers of people participated in the activities out of which the scenes emerged. Some growth is essential to create the levels of human interest and vitality required for articulation. Moreover, during the scene's golden age, growth continues at a steady rate. However, our primary focus is on the explosive expansion which eventually obliterates the scene. To fully understand this expansion, we must start from the beginning and trace the growth through various phases in the life of the scene.

DIRECT CONTACT AND WORD OF MOUTH

Surfing. In this case, diffusions of the scene only through direct contact and word of mouth lasted several years and proceeded very slowly. This was partly because very few people came into contact with surfing immediately after World War II. Most of the favorite surfing locations—Malibu, The Cove, Rincon, Secas, County Line, and Swamié's—were away from cities. Only Windansea and the Manhattan Pier were highly visible surfing locations.

At that time, too, surfboards were in short supply. When an interested person wanted to start surfing, he had to wait months to get the sport's one essential piece of equipment. Dale Velzey, the first surfboard manufacturer, did not start producing boards in volume until after 1954. Bob Simmons and the few others who made boards usually did so only for friends. Many people built their own boards, but this meant obtaining balsa wood, fiberglass, and resin, and then struggling with these these difficult and unfamiliar materials. (The outcome of this struggle was usually odd-looking, too.)

But around 1954 the corner was turned: In fact, two corners were turned simultaneously. Simmons and Velzey perfected the new fiberglass-coated balsa boards. Their relative lightness and maneuverability made it possible for surfers to ride the quicker-breaking waves normally found at places with sandy bottoms. This meant that most of the populated beaches, such as Hermosa and Manhattan, could be surfed, which gave the sport much more visibility.

Moreover, the vigorous expansion of activity gave a boost to the surfboard industry. Velzey moved·from under the pier to a shop nearby, and later to one in Malibu. He hired several of the young surfers to help produce the boards and installed Hap Jacobs in his own shop to do nothing but "glass" the boards shaped by Velzey and his helpers. Then Jacobs branched out on his own. Hobie, a surfer from the Laguna Beach-Dana Point area, also opened up a shop; others followed. By 1956, an aspiring surfer could walk into one of these shops and either walk out with a board or be assured of delivery of one within a couple of weeks.

The mass production of light boards opened up the sport to smaller, younger, and weaker surfers. There had always been a few of them surfing, but these few possessed a compensatory tenacity which was not required with the light board. For the first time, large groups of very young boys and significant numbers of girls entered the sport. By and large, until the middle fifties, the women who did spend any amount of time around the scene were wives and girl friends of surfers (though most of the surfers were loners), or perhaps some summer "groupies" following a particular surfing clique.

The Hippie Scene. There was very little time before the hippie scene moved beyond diffusion by word of mouth and direct contact, because various forms of the media pounced upon it almost immediately. But even in this short period—a few months at most—the news traveled fast and far. An intertwined and extended music, drug, and "new left" communication network already existed in the San Francisco Bay Area, rapidly carrying news of anything related to these phenomena. The buzzing about new drugs had been going out on the network for some time before more articulated hippie forms took shape in La Honda and the Haight-Ashbury, so the exciting news of "great new things" spread rapidly.

Like the surfing scene needed the new surfboard to expand, the hippie scene needed a new system of supply of its sine qua non, LSD. As mentioned earlier, by 1965 the Berkeley hip-chemists had broken the code and set up underground factories, so the drug was being dispersed widely in the Bay Area.

Other than specific information about new drugs or wild events, the informal communication networks spread a new collective mood, identity, or feeling of we-ness. The *we* was all the people who had been heavily into marijuana, folk music, and civil rights, and were dabbling—or willing to dabble—in LSD. Two anecdotes told to me by friends who were swept up into the emerging scene in those months capture this spreading collective feeling.

We were riding along in Bobby's panel truck in Marin County. We had all dropped acid and were just digging the countryside. All of a sudden Bobby spots this car full of crazies coming at us and we all waved to each other out the windows. So we stop and they stop and we get out of the car and frolic around in the field together. It was wild, we had never seen each other before. But we knew and they knew that we were into the same thing. I know they were high too. But nothing was ever said. We didn't even find out each others' names. We just grooved awhile and then got back in our cars and split.

I was walking down Haight pretty high, but not out of my skull, and I was walking past this house with several people sitting on the porch fooling around with different instruments. One was playing a flute and another a guitar. There were some congo drums sitting there, so I just walked up on the porch and sat down and started playing the drums. It was mellow. Nobody said anything at first, we just continued to play, slipping in and out of several tunes. Later that day we went inside and had something to eat and got high again. It was so natural and mellow.

THE MEDIA

Surfing. Around the mid-fifties, mass communication picked up surfing. First, several magazine articles appeared in skin diving and men's magazines, such as *True* and *Argosy*.[1] The effect these had on the expansion rate was probably limited. Soon, however, people from the surfing ranks themselves developed mass madia mechanisms for spreading the word which moved the scene into its first period of *rapid* growth. Bud Browne was the first to film surfing and show the films to his friends. Since everyone who saw them was excited and wanted more, Browne rented the Santa Monica High School Auditorium and showed a short film to an audience of about 200 surfers and their friends. The reception was enthusiastic, and several other surfers interested in photography started producing their own surfing films. John Severson and Bruce Brown especially made films which they showed all over California to growing, enthusiastic audiences. Surfing, as the international success of Bruce Brown's later film, "The Endless Summer," proved, has fantastic cinematic appeal.

The pattern in the surfing films produced and shown between 1955 and 1963 was approximately the same. The filmmaker showed and personally narrated sixteen mm color films of surf and surfing in California and Hawaii. As the producers presented the films over and over, they developed a humorous commentary replete with "in" surfing jokes. The audiences included active surfers, friends and families of surfers, and other high school youths from the beach cities who were developing an interest in the scene.

One way this internal media mechanism had a profound impact on the diffusion of surfing was by creating celebrities. The films usually focused on one or a few skilled surfers transported to the different surfing spots so that the film-maker would be assured of shooting quality surfing. These celebrities received the kind of recognition from adolescents formerly reserved for football players and other star high school athletes, and emulation of the celebrity surfers added greatly to surfing's appeal.

Finally, surfing broke big in the conventional media. First a best-selling novel, by Eugene Burdick, appeared. Called *The Ninth Wave,* it began in Hermosa Beach with as the young hero a teenage surfer waiting day after day in the hot sun for the "ninth wave" (which, the book inaccurately suggested, is the largest of a series of waves). The novel succeeded in capturing some of the lore of surfing and circulating it to a large audience. It was surpassed by another inaccurate mass media presentation of surfing which reached millions, particularly teenagers. A vacationing professor, Frederick Koehner, spent the summer of 1955 in Malibu, and his teenage daughter Susan became a part of the summer Malibu surfers' clique. Koehner turned her and his experiences into a novel (*Gidget*) which was quickly made into a movie (1957). The film in turn precipitated a number of magazine and newspaper articles on surfing.

The surfers got back into the growing media dissemination of surfing by publishing a variety of surfing magazines. John Severson, who had financed himself handsomely with the earlier films, introduced *The Surfer* (1960). It was an immediate success and was followed by other, less-successful imitators: *Surfing Illustrated* (Winter 1962); *Surf Guide* (Summer 1963); and *Petersen's Surfing Magazine* (December 1963). The magazines reached a much wider audience than the surfing films, since they were sold in every part of the United States, including the Midwest.

The magazines did not just spread the bare idea of surfing; they spread the surfing patterns by a variety of articles, stories, and jokes, through which the beginner could learn the basic language of surfing and a great deal about the fundamentals of board handling, wave riding, and behaving as a bona fide, "knobby kneed" surfer.[2] The films, with expert commentary by their narrators, had imparted some of the more or less subtle dimensions of surfing—both in wave riding and on shore.

Perhaps the media form which reached the widest audience, though it appeared quite late, was the pop music style which was attached to the skyrocketing scene to take advantage of its growing popularity. What became labelled surfing music was a corruption of the music which had become popular as background music to surfing films. John Severson started it by playing Henry Mancini's theme music to "Peter Gunn" behind his first film. Others quickly picked up this idea with a variety of different music types, even classical. But by 1960 or 1961, most of the films were using folk or rock and roll music, which seemed to complement the surfing sequences. This music became associated with surfing. Consequently, several Southern California musicians slightly converted their style, wrote some tunes with lyrics about surfing, and became "surfing bands." It worked. The Beach Boys, for instance, had several surfing songs in the top ten during 1962 and 1963.

Hippies. The first hippie dances, promoted by the Family Dog and Bill Graham, which were well publicized and which, when attended, imparted key elements of the emerging scene, were the first occasion on which the media got into disseminating the hippie scene. The acid tests of the Merry Pranksters also served for systematic attempts to spread word about the upcoming events. The producers distributed handouts and displayed art nouveau posters in appropriate locations, such as at the Berkeley campus, San Francisco State College, Telegraph Avenue, Haight-Ashbury, and North Beach. When these events clicked, the promoters used the radio and newspapers to spread word of subsequent dances. The Pranksters promoted the weekend Trips Festival with professional publicists who advertised the event through the newspapers and through a series of promotional stunts, like noon parades in San Francisco's financial district.

As soon as a sprinkling of "hip" merchants appeared on Haight Street, and the Haight was becoming identified with the emerging hippie lifestyle (1966), several underground newspapers devoted to the Haight and the hippie life appeared. *The Oracle* (October 1966) and *Good Times* (February 1968), which were the first and most prominent of these, were sold all over the city by young people trying to earn enough money to survive in the Haight. The *Berkeley Barb,* which had been established in June 1965 and which was slanted toward radical politics, was infiltrated by younger, hippie-oriented staff who leaned it toward the new hippie community. Eventually, a conflict developed between the younger, hip staff and the owner. The younger staff left and started *The Tribe* as a hip competitor to the *Barb. The Tribe,* along with the rest of the underground press (including the *Barb*), devoted much or most of its space to the hippie events and to observations of the world from the new hippie perspective. In this way, they contributed to the dissemination of the new scene.

These publications, however, were limited geographically. It was pop music which first carried the news of the new San Francisco lifestyle to the nation and the world. The San Francisco bands did not accomplish this, however. Their music was recorded, but in the first two years of the scene, the only hit from the local groups was the Jefferson Airplane's *Somebody to Love.* Nevertheless, news of the San Francisco developments raced through the music world, and other artists recorded songs about the scene and about San Francisco. Scott McKenzie's big hit—"If you're going to San Francisco, be sure to wear some flowers in your hair"— recorded in the spring of 1967, was the most important of these and was very significant in enlisting new members for the scene.

All of these media were instantly outstripped by conventional newspapers and magazines which discovered the hippies and pounced upon them with a speed and intensity unprecedented in the reporting of new, unconventional life-styles (much unlike their sluggish response to surfing). After the summer of 1966, which was the apogee of the short Golden Age, the San Francisco *Chronicle* sent its reporters to Haight-Ashbury to package this "new commodity" for distribution on the mass media market.[3] After the initial *Chronicle* stories and the positive identification of the new hippie scene, journalists from all over the nation descended upon the Haight, causing an immediate flood of articles. I made a chart of the articles on hippies listed in the *Publishers' Guide to Periodical Literature,* broken up over the four phases in the hippie scene (and including the Golden Age).

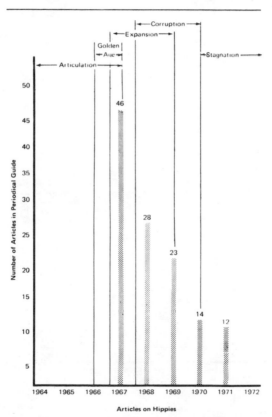

Articles on Hippies

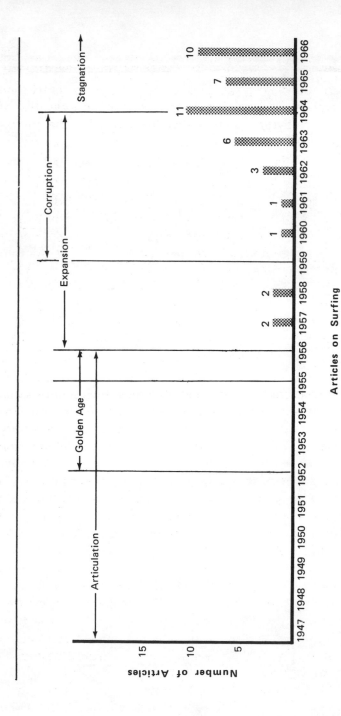

Articles on Surfing

The chart shows no gradual buildup—just a smash entry, and then a gradual decline. The pattern is as much indicative of society's sensitivity to alternative lifestyles by the middle 1960s as it is of the intrinsic newsworthiness of hippie scenes. Compare the attention to hippies in my second chart, showing the conventional media's treatment of surfers, which did not become at all intense until the mid 1960s, when the scene was already in its last stages. By the middle 1960s, of course, deviant lifestyles were highly salable, and journalists were alert to any new stirrings on the outer fringes of society. This posture made the media active participants in the growth and death of the deviant lifestyles. The deluge of articles on the hippies in 1967 and after precipitated a corresponding deluge of initiates to the new lifestyle and, thereby, altered and, in fact, irreparably damaged the scene.[4]

THE HIGH SCHOOL

The relationship of the scenes to most high school social systems was another important factor in their growth. The typical high school social system in the late 1950s and early 1960s was a fragile form which easily surrendered when threatened by an outside competitor. The system's fragility resulted from its inherent characteristics. It was dominated by a few highly popular youths who possessed esteemed skills, material accouterments, and personality attributes, and who were very active in maintaining their social ranking. Most youths in the system were either obsequious, low-status aspirants, or totally outside, either through ignorance of the system or by choice. Needless to say, there were few winners in this milieu. Most enviously and unhappily watched the leading crowd, the soshes, ostentatiously go about the business of having a great time. But this miserable system could only exist as long as there were no external, status-bestowing alternatives, which was the case until 1956.

Surfers. After 1955, in each of the high schools in the beach towns in Southern California, a small group of new male "weirdos" appeared. These were former "nobodies" (low-status youths, either from the ranks of outsiders or those youths oriented to the system but occupying a low position in it) who had let their sun-bleached or peroxided hair grow long and hang down over their eyes, wore "tennies," huaraches, or no shoes, and called themselves "surfers." The surfing identity and activities offered them an alternative to the cliquish high school social systems and the highly organized school athletic activities. Mickie Dora, who turned his back on the high school and began surfing at Malibu in the early 1950s, describes one of the great appeals of surfing.

> When I went to school damn near everything was organized. Little league baseball, stoop-tag, the three major sports . . . everything was concocted around the buddy system. They never left you alone. But with surfing I could go to the beach and not have to depend on anybody. I could take a wave and forget about it [*Surf Guide*, October 1963, p. 7].

As the surfers began to appear in one school after another—which developed near the coast and moved slowly inland—the local soshes either ignored or openly derogated them, and tried to keep them in a lower-status category which, according to the rules of the dominant system, was their rightful rank. In some schools, particularly those with a large working-class student body—such as Hawthorne and Torrance High Schools (which are located several miles inland from Hermosa Beach)—the surfers came into more open and sometimes violent conflict with the "greasers," "esses," or "bads," whom the surfers disparagingly called "hodads." Though they tended to run from violent confrontation with hodads, these first contingents of surfers held their ground in the high school setting. Surfing, after all, offered them material out of which to construct dignified alternative identities, a cohesive clique of their own, and a set of particularly exciting, physically dangerous, and, thereby, "masculine" athletic activities.

After their demonstration of solidarity—and after surfing started receiving outside attention—the surfers' numbers in particular schools grew. At first they opened up a pocket between the soshes and the hoods, and then they chipped away at both strata above and below. Eventually there was, in every school, a mass exodus to the ranks of surfers, leaving only thin top and bottom layers. Finally, most of the soshes themselves, high school athletes and their girl friends, converted to surfing. Few hard-core hoods got involved in surfing, however.

This conversion of one high school after another proceeded slowly at first, accelerating as surfing moved inland and as community awareness increased. By 1961 and 1962, many inland Los Angeles high schools were penetrated and converted to surfing in a single, usually the spring semester,

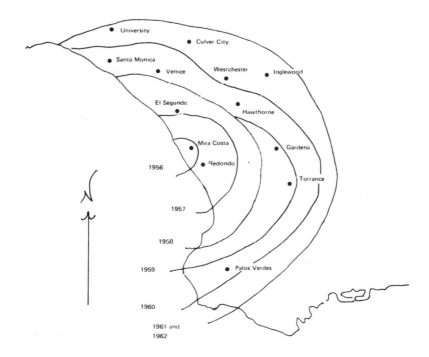

when the summer beach season was approaching. My third chart traces the approximate dispersion of surfing through Los Angeles high schools. From Los Angeles, the dispersion continued to high schools up and down the coast and then jumped across country to the East Coast. Obviously the effect this had on surfing was one of thousands of youths pouring simultaneously onto the beaches to join the scene.

Hippies. Having been upset by one outside competitor, the California high school systems remained particularly unstable. The old leading types were able to temporarily reestablish local status hierarchies in 1963 or 1964 by incorporating surfing into the normal round of high school activities. Once many football and basketball players and other high school athletes had shown themselves to be excellent surfers, being a surfer gave no special distinction.

However, after 1964, the lower ranks remained less subservient. In elementary school they had witnessed the revolt of the nobodies, and they were cognizant of the possibility of escaping the local system by turning to outside scenes. Local high-status participants also had to keep a sharp eye on outside developments because they did not want to get caught short, as their predecessors had.

Consequently, after two tranquil years (1965 and 1966), another alternative scene sprang up in San Francisco. The low-status, middle-strata youth—both male and female—did not waste time; they dropped what they were doing and flocked to Haight-Ashbury. The high-status soshes, though they did not leave the school and migrate to the Haight, grew full heads of hair (if the high school coaches would permit), smoked marijuana, dressed in the new hip styles, and strenuously avoided the label "straight."

As in the case of surfing, the major consequence of this process for the scene was that in a short time period the scene was deluged with escapees from the high school social systems. This time it happened more quickly, in a vastly larger geographical sphere—extending to all parts of the country—and, consequently, it involved many more high school youths.

CORRUPTION

The surfing and hippie scenes could not absorb the thousands of persons who stampeded to them. In both cases, the incoming crowds mangled the original spontaneous moods, friendly interactional patterns, and refined cultural forms. The process of corruption was inevitable because the lifestyles which could be successfully pursued by a relatively small number of surfers or hippies, were simply not possible when the numbers were multiplied many times. Other processes which compounded the corruption followed. The old-timers grew resentful of newcomers, whom they derogated; and there was an intense concern over authenticity which eventually produced gross exaggerations of the original patterns.

OVERCROWDING

Surfing. Crowds created concrete problems in surfing, the most serious in wave riding itself. Ideally, only one surfer should ride each wave (two if the wave can be ridden both left and right). When there are five or six surfers at a particular surfing spot which has one reef or one wave location, the sport becomes much less enjoyable and, in fact, a little dangerous. Beginning surfers are particularly bothersome. They cannot maneuver well in the water; consequently they get in the way of others and lose their surfboards more often.[5]

When the crowds swelled in surfing, the preferred surfing spots were virtually impossible to ride. When there were good waves at Malibu, Rincon, Secas, Windansea, Swami's, or any of the well-known, high-quality surfing locations, there would be dozens—perhaps hundreds—of surfers in the water from sunrise to sunset. Four, five, six, or more surfers would take off on every wave, pushing, shoving, cutting in front of each other, and ruining the ride for all. Even the beaches with the sort of surf that spreads over the length of the beach became so crowded that much of the enjoyment of surfing was lost.

Out of the water, great numbers of surfers also created problems. Many of the surfing spots were in front of private land, which surfers had to cross. This created no problem when there were small numbers of surfers, but when hundreds stamped across someone's private property and hung around the private beaches (or even public beaches, for that matter), local citizens began to complain. This resulted in the closing of many of the accesses to surfing spots. "Cottons," a surfing spot directly in front of the Cotton Ranch in San Clemente (later to become "the Western White House"), was one of these. Local communities took general steps to curb surfing by closing many public beaches to wave riding, or by restricting the hours such beaches could be surfed.

Moreover, the summertime movement of thousands of surfers to the beach towns had a drastic impact. Local citizens in the Los Angeles and San Diego beach communities could accept a limited number of unproductive individuals, but when thousands began sleeping on beaches and in cars, crowding into rented houses and apartments, shoplifting, and littering, the local citizenry was outraged. Surfers began to experience negative sanctions, such as harassment and arrests by police, and evictions from residences.

Hippies. In a similar, but exaggerated fashion, the hoards of hippie newcomers created concrete problems for the Haight-Ashbury. Prior to the summer of 1967, a manageable number of unproductive, full-time hippies were walking the streets and sharing residences in the community. The invasion during the summer of 1967 immediately altered that.

The hippie community was well aware beforehand that the summer onslaught was imminent. In fact, the HIP (Haight Independent Proprietors) merchants—the owners and managers of shops which catered to hippies or sold hippie-style commodities—actively encouraged the invasion by advertising "the summer of love." There were several meetings of the merchants, the Diggers, and interested Haight residents to plan programs for handling the summer flood. They even requested help from the city administration, though officials quickly refused since the city did not want to encourage an invasion of long-haired, unproductive, impecunious, unwashed drifters—with or without flowers in their hair.

Several programs to handle the summer crowds were implemented by the established hippies and others who were developing an interest in the Haight community. Three of the most prominent were (1) the Haight Switchboard, which offered 24-hour referral for a wide variety of services, such as temporary housing, medicine, free food, etc.; (2) Huckleberry House, for juvenile runaways; and (3) the Haight Free Medical Clinic, established by the doctors at the nearby University of California Medical School who had been interested in drugs, particularly the new psychedelics. The Diggers, who operated a free food outlet and store, increased their services. All of these were not enough to guarantee a summer of love.

In the first place, the problem of crowding was similar to that which plagued the surfers. But for the hippies the problem was exaggerated because the area involved was much smaller. In the Haight in the summer of 1967, the crash pads proliferated and were jammed with so many youths that at night there was wall-to-wall sleeping or fornicating. Sleeping hippies nightly filled the Panhandle and Golden Gate Park, which formed boundaries of the Haight. The food problem was more than the Diggers or other free food services could handle. The huge numbers milling in the streets and the park constituted a constant throng, around which the buses on Haight Street had to be rerouted.

Indigent crowds of this size produce problems even if they are orderly and abstinent, which was hardly the case with the new hippies, who were heavy drug users, sexually active, and relatively unruly. So without any other behavior or processes to compound the situation, the crowding itself produced serious health, cleanliness, and public order problems. In addition, the hippie communal spirit, and the close, friendly, face-to-face interactional patterns which had sprung from the LSD experience and the early scene's dynamics, impossible to sustain among a constant throng, disappeared. This inconsistent and ambivalent statement by a resident of Morningstar Ranch reflects the strain and impossibility of loving everyone on the street.

> I would go out for a whole day, just meet fifty or sixty people, and just talk to them for five minutes or an hour and eat with them and get loaded with them and just have a really groovy, groovy time. And at the end of a day you have this feeling inside you, this love feeling that just can't be expressed. And like to me, once you experience that, like there's no room for any kind of hatred. Like people are people and they have moods and sometimes they do things that they don't want to do. You know, I'd like to be all good, but I can't—you know what I mean?
>
> Well, like I've said, everybody has their moods and things like that. It's hard for everybody to be kind to each other. It's like giving a lot, if you know what I mean. you don't have to give material things—food and clothing, which does help, but just like friendship on the streets to everbody [Lewis Yablonsky, 1968, pp. 187-188].

Every crowd, even a hippie crowd, has unfriendly, hostile, threatening individuals. The Haight had a majority of black residents when the hippies moved in, and many young, working- or lower-class black youths were openly resentful toward these middle-class whites who were rejecting the lifestyle to which the black youth aspired, and who were voluntarily dabbling in poverty. One day when I passed a small corner grocery store one block off Haight Street I witnessed a black youth hit a hippie in the face and knock him down without saying a word after the hippie had asked him for some spare change. Besides hostile black youths, there were many hippies "on bummers" from drugs or just from the vicissitudes of moods. As if this were not enough, working-class youths from other parts of the city wanted to be around the action, but did not subscribe to the hippie lifestyle. The Hell's Angels never fully adopted the love ethic, but established themselves on Haight Street and regularly mistreated hippies. Lewis Yablonsky, in his study of hippies, observed some of the exploitative, aggressive activities of the Angels.

> They ruled many hippies who came near them by inflicting a subtle terror. I personally felt this as I hovered around them at a pizza parlor on Haight Street after Chocolate George's funeral. One very greasy, leering member of the Angels accosted me for a quarter to "get across the bridge." His demeanor let me know that it would be wise for me to cooperate with his simple request. I wasn't at all interested in testing him and his friends.
>
> The Angels commandeered what they wanted. Two Angels who were standing around hugging each other and rapping in loud voices were being entertained on the street. A long-robed; beaded, Christ-like hippie played his flute—apparently exclusively for their enjoyment and amusement. He stopped at one point to talk to a passing friend. The Angel turned to him, broke the stride of his discussion, and commanded, "Hey, man, play that fuckin' flute—I like it." The two Hell's Angels decided to go down the block to see a friend and the flutist was commanded to follow along and provide music for their walk [pp. 204-205] .

So instead of finding a community of sharing, loving, flower children living an exciting, spontaneous new lifestyle, most of the 1967 arrivals found a throng of people like themselves who did not know each other, did not have a place to sleep, not enough food, few resources, and nothing much to do except mill around and try to stay high.

AUTHENTICITY

Surfing. As the problems of crowding grew, a negative attitude toward newcomers in surfing emerged. The derogatory concepts "kook"—the despicable beginner—and "pseudo surfer"—an individual who could not or did not surf, but flocked in great numbers to the scene's on-land territories and called himself a surfer—appeared and were loosely tossed about. This severe derogation of the newcomer precipitated an intense concern over authenticity in the scene. Most surfers who commingled in surfing territories did not know each other and only in the water, by demonstrating surfing skill, could it be established for sure that one was not a kook or pseudo surfer.

Surfing had already become very competitive and skill-conscious. In the middle 1950s, wave-riding styles, which were steadily improving, shifted from "making waves" to "hot dogging," a surfing style characterized by sharp turns, "walking to nose," "hanging five" (placing the foot, and thereby the five toes, on the nose of the board as it crosses the wave), and other radical maneuvers. Status in the scene had always been largely based on surfing skill. When the problems of crowds and the derogation of the newcomer began to appear, the competitiveness related to surfing skill was greatly increased.

Competitiveness was not restricted to the water, for surfers met other surfers more out of the water than in. Proving one's authenticity was therefore an ongoing problem. Only a few celebrities were known by sight, so that they never had to worry over their legitimate status in the scene. One effect of this concern over status was the stifling of spontaneity and experimentation. Most members, whose relative status was not assured, felt that it was unwise to take chances by experimenting with new patterns. It was safer to learn and follow the accepted patterns well. Only the scene's recognized leaders dared innovate, and most other persons imitated their surfing techniques, board and dress styles, and speech patterns. Consequently, the range of variations in the scene narrowed considerably.

Hippies. By the end of the summer of 1967, most people in the Haight scene were in agreement that the summer of love had been a "bummer" and that the major problem was just too many newcomers. As they had in surfing, the new arrivals—the "plastic" or "instant hippies"—became pariahs of the scene. At the end of the summer, a former member of the San Francisco Mime Troupe organized a funeral for the hippie era. It wound down Haight Street in a futile attempt to terminate the scene. The owners of the Psychedelic Shop—the first hippie store—closed and left a sign in the window which reflected the negative attitude t.woard the flood of newcomers: "Nebraska Needs You More."

The same nervousness over authenticity that had appeared in surfing also showed up in the hippie scene. However, the hippies had no technique such as wave riding for discriminating authenticity.

It was never quite clear what a hippie really was, and at this time many persons were moving out of the Haight and disassociating themselves from the label. But the Haight was still full and many people continued to visit or migrate to it. Moreover, the hippie scene was spreading all over the country, particularly to New York's Greenwich Village.

Competitiveness subplanted the original friendly mood of the Haight. Of course, the bare problems of overcrowding—the problems related to food shortage, poor hygiene, sexual promiscuity, and homelessness—had already soured the mood considerably, but I believe it was the derogation of the newcomer and the resultant concern over authenticity that completely tripped the scene over from "good vibrations" to "bad vibrations," from love to hostility.

As in surfing, both the concern over authenticity and the increased competitiveness drastically reduced the scene's spontaneity. The best evidence of this is the disappearance of dancing at the rock dances. At the first series of dances in 1965, everyone danced. One of their most remarkable facets was that people who had *never* danced before danced all night. The dances were filled with people doing their own steps, crude as they were. Then, as the scene developed, a group of nondancers, who sat on the floor near the rock band, appeared. By 1967, this group had grown steadily larger, but after the summer of 1967, the nondancers crowded out the dancers. Finally, dancing virtually disappeared. People's concern to be unobtrusive and not to look foolish had become too pervasive to permit the earlier collective, effusive expressions.

In general, the scene became conformist in developing a characteristic speech, dress, and hair styles. An easily identifiable costume, grooming style, and manner of speech emerged and were imitated by most persons who wanted to avoid being considered unauthentic. The costume included blue jeans; straight, long hair (though black and Jewish "naturals" were acceptable); leather jackets with lots of tassels or fringe; leather pants; beads; Indian headbands; and sandals or boots. The lexicon was reduced to so few phrases that hippie conversations became unintelligible. Sophisticated speculation into philosophy and experimentation in new art forms, even in music, ceased among the rank and file. Only the established leaders could afford to venture into new avenues of thought or art. The nervous hippie masses followed along.

EXAGGERATIONS

Surfing. Overcrowding eventually led to a more radical corruption of surfing. Newcomers had expected to be well received in this alternative life style, and perhaps even earn some recognition for their bold rejection of conventional systems. They discovered, however, that they were unwelcome and seen as contaminating the scene. Some of these new arrivals, of course, were not satisfied with this arrangement and aspired to immediate higher status.

To become a fully authentic member, however, it was necessary to become a competent wave rider, and this required at least a year of hard work. To become a celebrity required much more time, considerable natural ability, and some luck (you had to appear in the films, or win surfing contests to become widely known). Unsatisfied with a slow, uncertain course to the top, the more ambitious newcomers cut a different path to membership and, in the case of the most adventurous, to fast fame by learning and conspicuously demonstrating the most obvious attributes of the scene.

This process took the scene in a bizarre and deviant direction. Since the newcomers were from the scene's media audience, the attributes of which they were most aware were those reported in the media. In the business of packaging and selling attention-getting phenomena, the mass media elected to emphasize the most bizarre and deviant aspects of the scene. Often they distorted or reshaped them to make them appear even more bizarre and deviant. In the case of an alternative lifestyle like the surfing scene, this media bias is enhanced by the perceptions of local citizens and some political figures, who tell the media their own slanted views and are more willing to believe and watch media versions which use, and are consistent with, their own biased views of the scene. In the case of surfing, several types of bizarre activities got considerable attention from the local citizenry and the media and were, therefore, becoming essential components in the outsider's conception of surfing.

Surfing parties were much like the parties of most young people, with drinking, noise, and some fornication. When the numbers of surfers in a given place got high enough so that the parties were frequent and overflowing, outsiders saw the surfers as engaged in a constant debauch. In remote surfing spots, surfers were very careless about changing their clothes and were nude for a few moments in the transition from

swimming suits to street clothes. While this could be perceived as perfectly conventional in small groups, on a larger scale
on a populated beach it had to be perceived differently.
Likewise, fire building on remote beaches is normal and can
be tolerated, but on a public beach, perhaps in front of
expensive homes, a fire is a nuisance and probably illegal. So
the image of surfing which formed in the minds of the
conventional cummunity and was emphasized by the media
was one of deviance and abandon. And this image was in the
minds of ambitious newcomers who wanted to become part
of the upper ranks of surfing. Many newer surfers began to
exaggerate bizarre and deviant activities, to a great extent for
outside audiences, which they perceived as highly irritated by
surfing. Consequently, they executed new forms of abandon
less for the satisfaction of the activities themselves, or to
perform for other surfers, but more with antagonism, with
the intention of even further irritating this outside audience.

Many forms of genital exhibitionism appeared, to some
extent because of their power to amuse the surfers, but more
because of their ability to antagonize the audience. For
instance, one morning a small group on a surfing excursion to
Malibu Colony, a spot in front of very expensive homes,
stripped to put on their swimsuits. A middle-aged woman
yelled from the balcony of one of the homes for them to
stop displaying themselves. The surfers stopped putting on
their trunks, shouted obscene expletives and shook their
penes at her. She called the police, which was of course a
futile gesture. When they arrived, there were so many surfers
in the water that identification of the offenders was
impossible.

A unique and bizarre form of exhibitionism—the
"brown eye"—developed out of a surfing maneuver called a
"head dip" and spread throughout the beach communities.
The surfing maneuver was accomplished by a bend at the
waist while facing the wall of a wave being surfed. The
"brown eye head dip" was a head dip during which the surfer

pulled his trunks down, showing his backside to those on shore. The "brown eye" (called "mooning" in other contexts) was repeated increasingly in public places. In 1959 and 1960, in the beach towns around Los Angeles or San Diego, a youth's bare buttocks, framing the side window of a passing car, was a common sight.

As mentioned earlier, fire building became a display of abandon. Not only did surfers start fires on beaches where fires were not permitted, they burned almost any material in the area—like picket fences, shacks, and lifeguard stands. In one case, some surfers lighted the pilings of a railroad trestle, although they did put them out before the trestle was burned.

Surfing parties became notorious for their abandon. Extreme drunkenness, sexual promiscuity, fighting, and physical damage to property were the results of a good surfing party. Indeed parties achieved memorable status by the degree of destruction they inflicted.

Styles of personal grooming became even more bizarre. Hair got longer. Old, oversized overcoats were worn over bathing suits in the winter. Surfing trunks many sizes too big—called "baggies"—were worn while surfing.

Nazi symbols like the swastika and iron cross revealed more antagonism than most of the other patterns. These symbols, which had been introduced to the Los Angeles surfers in a surfing film, first had implications of comedy as we saw earlier. They were displayed on surfboards, cars, walls, or any flat surface near surfing spots, and worn as amulets. No surfer I interviewed in this period revealed any degree of knowledge of the historical, racist, or fascist significance of the symbols. Surfers had seized on them merely because they discovered that the symbols could antagonize outsiders.

Formerly, female surfers were either the girl friends of surfers or female athletes who participated in the sport. Later female surfers—or at times nonsurfers—attached themselves to the scene and participated in the deviant activities. These females were often sexually promiscuous, and those who actually surfed matched the males' brown eyes with the "bare tittie." (Some of them became notorious for their public execution of "brown eye" as well.)

Theft also increased in this phase. Surfers have big appetities and little money. To the aggravation of the many small grocers located near surfing spots, shoplifting was common. So was surfboard theft. To some extent, the youths who stole boards had backgrounds in organized stealing, and they recognized the profit potential in fencing surfboards.

As a consequence of all this, the irresponsible, untrammeled, and uncomplicated spirt of surfing was converted by the newcomers to a spirit of complete abandon, or, more accurately stated, to one of the conspicuous *display* of abandon. Once this trend started, it spread throughout the ranks of surfing, even to those old timers who did not want to be left behind on any new trend. In some ways, the abandon had begun as an extension of the comedy aspects we described earlier, but the purposive display of abandon was now directed toward the larger society and was more expressive of antagonism than of play. During the early 1960s, this abandon became surfing's trademark, especially in Los Angeles and San Diego counties. To the majority of the population, the surfer was just another type of delinquent.

Hippies. The first exaggerations of hippie traits were early in the expansion of the scene. Newcomers did not have the prior experience with bohemian or other deviant patterns which would have prepared them for the problems that emerge when conventional structures and norms are rejected. Consequently, they naively and excessively embraced the hippie ethic—particularly its value on tolerance—and escalated it to a socially malfunctional level. When a neighborhood became overcrowded and the group living situations in it intolerable, it was virtually impossible for hippies groups to accomplish the minimum tasks necessary for orderly group life. "Do your own thing" meant shun all social responsibilities and put down anyone who tried to organize collective action. The offensive problems which resulted from the breakdown of group responsibility were epidemic in the Haight. Houses occupied by hippies were often filthy and seriously damaged. The littering and general abuse turned Haight-Ashbury into one of the ugliest, dirtiest neighborhoods in the city. There were serious interrelated problems of health and hygiene, caused by the hippies' failure to keep themselves, their houses, and the area clean, or to follow a minimal health regimen (not to mention the aggravation of drug abuse).

Perhaps the mistreatment of young children, who as infants were often given little more than birth so that their lives could be "natural," best demonstrates the detrimental exaggeration of the original hang-loose ethic. Lewis Yablonsky visited Morningstar Ranch, a hippie haven, and reported two typical examples of child neglect.

> As we were talking I felt compelled to switch off my tape recorder and attend to a little blond child about four, who was wandering aimlessly about and crying. It wore a long green velvet gown that was filthy. The pathetic baby had one shoe on and one shoe missing. No one seemed to pay any attention to it. It appeared abandoned.

> I went over and picked the baby up and hugged it. I became aware that the child smelled badly from urine and feces. I hugged it again. The little baby and I looked into each other's eyes and I'll never forget the child's simple words, "I'm lonely."

> I asked someone about the child's parents and received a matter-of-fact reply that the baby's mother was "out in the woods freaked-out on acid."

> I resumed my conversation with the young man as the baby stumbled up the hill. I told him:

> LY-That thing got to me. This little kid is wandering around aimlessly. It is all wet and dirty. You know what the kid said to me, "I'm lonely." These kids are really not taken care of, are they?

P-A-Kid got run over yesterday. His mother had taken acid and she had left him with someone—she didn't know who. He was run over by a car, a dog bit him, and he was taken to the hospital. He's back today and fortunately, he's still alive [pp. 188-189].

When the competitiveness stemming from concern over authenticity swept through the scene, the exaggeration of drug patterns followed. In the scene's articulation, the emphasis was on mind-expanding, psychedelic drugs. Other drugs, particularly speed and opiates, had been considered antithetical to the true spirit of the hippie life. However, in the expansion phase, greater numbers of people used first speed and then heroin.[6] There are at least two reasons for this, both related to the concern over authenticity. Newcomers trying to establish themselves, conspicuously displayed the scene attributes as they understood them. Often this led to choosing the escalation of drug use as a method to climb out of the lowly status of "instant" hippie. The negative implications of some drugs had no strong effect on them because their knowledge of the more subtle values of the scene was nil. So they proceeded on the course of demonstrating they were serious members of the scene by using drugs which were generally viewed as more dangerous and deviant.

The second reason that the newcomers turned to speed and heroin was that these drugs are easier to use in a hostile environment. In order to fully enjoy psychedelics, even marijuana, it is necessary to be surrounded by somewhat sympathetic, or at least, not hostile and threatening, people. "Bad trips" are often the result of a hostile social environment. Speed, with its hyped up euphoria (though paranoia does tend to set in after excessive use), and heroin, which removes the user from all concern over the attitudes of others, are the most suitable drugs in an unsympathetic, unfriendly, and threatening ambience. This is what the Haight was becoming during and after the summer of 1967, and the problem of speed and heroin exploded in the neighborhood.

The mounting hostilities in the Haight escalated and led to serious riots and violence after 1967. These new, very unhippie-like patterns were indirectly related to the increased corruption and competitiveness of the scene. The scene now drew many people who were not oriented to loving all their fellow human beings. The Hell's Angels—though the "Frisco" Angels were less belligerent than their Oakland brothers— never were completely comfortable with soft, more loving interrelationships, and they continued to occasionally shove and stomp hippies. As the mellow mood which had formerly characterized the scene gave way to more hostility and self-ishness, predatory, violent individuals began fiercely preying on the hippies. Many of these individuals were young black males who hated the white, middle-class poverty volunteers, and began to circulate among the hippies to obtain drugs, money, good times, and sex. Emmett Grogan describes some of the activities of these black youths.

Soon after the "hippie" street population thinned out a bit, gangs of didy-boppin', black bloods from all over the city began vamping through Haight-Ashbury seeking out "flower children" as prey. But most of them had already gone, making the women of the community the only easy marks for the black youths' blind reactionary acts of rape and robbery against anyone white. Their targets were always the weak, helpless and harmless girls who still thought of flowers as lovely and were attacked simply because they were accessible in the low-income neighborhood. This made the men of the community plenty fucking angry, and there was a series of fights, stabbings and shootings, until it looked like the whole goddamn thing was going to erupt into a race war with the "longhaired, shaggie honkies" led by the Frisco Hells Angels on one side against the "back-stabbin', women killin' niggers" led by some cats from the Fillmore who identified themselves as "Black Panthers." The cops intended to stand on the sidelines and wait for everyone to beat everyone else to death or at least into exhaustion, before they moved themselves in for the overkill of both sides [Grogan, pp. 516-518].

All the violence was not interracial. In an incident which reflects the general violent mood in the Haight at this time, a group of seven men and three women, all white, dragged a young female newcomer into an apartment one block off Haight Street, raped, beat, mutilated, and finally murdered her by kicking in her skull.

A great deal of violence in this final stage of the scene's corruption was related to a mixture of traditional hoodlum activities, and the escalation of drug use among the hippies. After the shift to heroin, the drug traffic changed from a friendly, orderly exchange to a rapacious, vindictive business. Since the young, white, middle-class youths had not entered drug use from an earlier route which included some stealing or hustling, they now had no way to support their heroin addiction. In addition, they were unprepared for the unscrupulous heroin-pushing patterns, and very often they were cheated by the older drug dealers who considered them legitimate prey. The hippies themselves began "burning"— that is, taking money without giving anything back—each other and other drug addicts. They also retaliated when they were burned, which resulted in a rash of shootings and killings. In general, violent crimes in the Haight rose to extreme levels, even to the extent that the neighborhood of love and flowers became one of the homicide centers of the city in 1968 and 1969.[7]

STAGNATION

As corruption proceeded, the scenes' old timers began to dislike what they saw happening. This negative image spread throughout the ranks. When it reached the outlying sources of newcomers, it halted them from joining the scene, and growth ceased. Many old timers left, as did some newer recruits. The scenes themselves did not disappear, however. Many people developed a relatively permanent orientation to the styles and, though they somewhat shifted their activities and attitudes, they struggled to maintain a general orientation. In addition, some maturing young people always remained unhappy with the other social worlds available to them and continued to gravitate to surfing and the hippie scene. Finally, many former members of these scenes continued to be influenced by their patterns. So these Grand Scenes, though they will never re-achieve the vitality and the spirit they once had, continue to exist in a state of *stagnation.*

DEFECTION

Surfing. As early as the beginning of the expansion, many old-time surfers had begun leaving the scene in disgust. At first the crowded surfing conditions made it impossible for them to enjoy the sport. Then they felt revulsion and resentment toward the corruptions of earlier surfing patterns and practices. For example, a magazine interview with Lance Carson, a surfer well known for nose-riding and generally excellent surfing at Malibu and Rincon, closes with this summary statement:

> Lance is a dedicated surfer who feels that wave ridin', is an art form in addition to being a sport. However, he views the future of surfing with concern but also with a feeling of futility. Because of the "explosion" in the surfing population while the number of surfing areas is actually decreasing due to thoughtless and selfish actions of a few misguided status seekers, he fears the sport is "done for" unless serious surfers organize to deal with the problem and attempt, before it is too late, to preserve this noble sport [*Surfing Illustrated*, Fall 1963, p. 62].

These statements, which were typical of those being made by established surfers at the time, are particularly instructive because they represent the attitudes of *Lance Carson*. Carson, more than any other individual, led surfing in bizarre and deviant directions. He became notorious in 1959, when he first entered surfing and had not yet learned to surf well, for his abandoned behavior. I witnessed him perform many brown eyes, one in front of an audience leaving a surfing movie. A few evenings after this, several people told me that he had walked into Mitchel's Donut Shop in Hermosa Beach, the local surfers' hangout, dropped his pants, put a donut on his penis, walked out, climbed on the hood of a friend's car, and was driven off into the night. That summer, 1959, he earned the nickname, "no-pants Lance." Not only was he blamed for many creative, exhibitionist acts, such as performing brown eyes for the passengers of the trains which pass many surfing locations between San Diego and San Francisco, but for the destruction through arson of many shacks near surfing spots.

His conversion to a more modest version of surfing epitomized the growing disdain in 1963 for the deviant acts of surfers. The defection accelerated, and soon many of the newcomers themselves were realizing that the benefits they had been seeking—either through participation in an exciting sport, or through a position in an alternative, status-bestowing system—had evaporated. They too began to defect, and the scene emptied out.

Hippies. In the autumn of 1967, many of the old-time hippies (if being a hippie for a year or two made one an old timer) fled from Haight-Ashbury. However, their abandonment was different from the earlier defection from surfing. The first veteran surfers who defected, though they may have continued to surf occasionally, quit the scene entirely; that is, they went to work, back to school, or in some other way took up a conventional lifestyle. The first hippie defectors were still deeply immersed in the hippie ethic and blamed the scene's corruption on the crowded Haight-Ashbury, not on the lifestyle. Many merely moved somewhere else, such as the Noe Valley area in San Francisco, which, like the Haight had been, was a neighborhood in transition, offering low rents in spacious, wood frame houses, and flats. However, others interpreted the corruption as a problem of dense American urban living and headed away from the city completely.

This migration was in three different directions. The first was to "forest crash pads." Hippie idealists took the hangloose ethic into the trees and mountains, where they believed it could be fully actualized: the mountains of Big Sur, Lou Gottlieb's Morningstar Ranch—a few miles north of San Francisco—and the rolling hills of Sonoma and Mendocino counties. Dozens of outdoor crash pads sprang up, where the flower children naively frolicked, stayed high, and quickly learned that the problems of filth, VD, hepatitis, bad vibes, violence, and hunger are not exclusive to the city. Yablonsky gave a good description of the failure of the forest crash pads in *The Hippie Trip.*

The second part of the migration was to other areas in the United States—the Midwest or New England—or to the less commercial cities of Europe and Asia. Hippies who migrated to these places believed that the problem of the Haight were peculiar to San Francisco.

The third part of the migration was to communes in rural areas, mostly in Northern California, and involved re-establishing pre-urban, cooperative, total living experiments which incorporated many hippie patterns, particularly drug use. Most of these communes did not fare much better than the forest crash pads because adherence to the hippie ethic made social organization and task accomplishment difficult, if not impossible.

The early defection took another, more radical form. A growing number of people who had, perhaps painfully, endured the relatively chaotic and traditionless life for months or years, rebounded toward tighter social structures and sacred traditions, and embraced one of the newer religious sects, such as the Hare Krishnas or one of the groups called Jesus Freaks, which were emerging among ex-hippies.

In the Haight, the numbers slacked off between October 1967 and May 1968. This, however, was also a result of many part-time hippies returning to school. Moreover, the Bay Area campus radical activities were cranking up again, and many of

the youths who alternated between radicalism and bohemianism returned to political involvement. Many participated in a minor student strike at San Francisco State and began planning to demonstrate at the upcoming Democratic National Convention in Chicago. The next season brought the big San Francisco State strike, then the People's Park demonstrations. But still newcomers and many part-timers poured into the neighborhood in the summer of 1968. The negative conception of the scene, the drug addiction, disease, and violence, however, had reached such levels that it was virtually impossible to pretend that anyone was having a good time. At this point, many tenacious Haight dwellers tried to develop a concept of hippies as the new oppressed minority, but since most people saw them as middle-class volunteers for poverty, this did not catch on. The defection increased, and finally, as it had in the case of surfing, the negative perception of the Haight and the hippie life reached back to the fountains of newcomers. The influx was shut off or considerably shut down.

BECOMING CONVENTIONAL

Surfing. Not all surfers defected. Many maintained a full-time commitment, but changed their life routines and attempted to change the patterns and image of surfing. Interviews similar to the one with Lance Carson, quoted above, were appearing in the surfing magazines and conventional media, and respected surfers exhorted other surfers to stop all the nonsense and clean surfing's dirty face. This widespread edifying impulse brought back the old, prewar, "respectable" surfing organizations. As early as 1961, a group of established surfers, several of whom had been members of the conventional surfing clubs before World War II and had come back to surfing when it developed into a big scene in the late 1950s, organized the United States Surfing Association. This organization reached a peak of about 3,000 members in

1963, and had as its primary purpose the restoration of surfing's corroding image and the salvation of many threatened surfing spots. Small surfing clubs reappeared after 1960, and by 1963 there was a club at almost every surfing spot in California.

These small clubs also participated in the *conventionalization* of surfing. Besides the "organized" surfers, a class of "professionals" began to replace the earlier, unconventionally oriented surfers. The professional surfer was a person who succeeded in two general ways in developing from surfing an economically viable and legal lifestyle. One way was to exploit one's surfing skills by selling one's celebrity status or by winning surfing contests. When surfing was recognized as having market potential, a few manufacturers, especially clothing manufacturers, hired surfers to advertise their products. However, only a few surfers made any significant money in this way and then only for a few years. The "professional" contests which appeared in 1964 supported another few surfers. At first, contests—which had started in Hawaii with the Makaha (1954) and began to multiply after the first surfing contest in Huntington Beach, California (1959)—were strictly amateur events. But when outside commercial interests discovered surfing, many businesses began sponsoring contests and offering cash prizes. For a few years, a handful of surfers (often the same ones who were earning money in the commercials) won enough money to qualify as "professionals."

Many surfers were supported by the industries which grew up in and around surfing. Surfboards, movies, magazines, swimsuits, and "wet suits" were produced and distributed largely by surfers. Several times existing businesses attempted to penetrate this rich market, especially the surfboard end of it, but they seemed unable to follow the subtle and shifting design preferences. Nor could they discover a method to mass produce boards that satisfied surfers. Only in the production of clothing, mainly bathing suits, did any nonsurfer commercial interest succeed in capitalizing on surfing commodities.

Of course, the popular music industry made money for a short period on surfing rock and roll, but as we argued earlier this was more of an adjustment of existing rock and roll music than something which developed out of surfing. Most of the surfing commercial enterprises still supported a large number of surfers, particularly surfboard manufacture, which is still controlled almost totally by surfers.

Hippies. There was no comparable organizing trend in the hippie scene, nor any explicit drive toward conventionalizing hippies. The hippie belief system, which was at the core of the lifestyle and which was in its essence totally unconventional, precluded this. Despite this, there was a definite shift toward the conventional in the hippie scene. Many people continued to cling to facets of the hippie lifestyle and identity—that is, they dressed in the hippie style and maintained such hippie patterns as using drugs, listening to rock music, and engaging in new offshoot fads (e.g., natural foods and astrology). But they returned to work or school, and to some extent accommodated to the conventional society. Those communes which managed to endure abandoned their strong anti-organizational bias and developed a relatively specific and rigid division of labor, and a normative system. In doing so, they departed from the hippie brand of unconventionality.

A more important trend toward the conventional was an outgrowth of hippie "capitalism," which eventually supported a large number of full-time, professional hippies. There had from the outset been hippie commercial enterprises; in fact, Haight-Ashbury did not become the hippie center until a few hippie shops were located on Haight Street. Following these stores were the underground newspapers, whose sale supported (at the poverty level) hundreds of hippies. The music also supported hundreds (many in a grander style), either in the bands or in the various positions around the bands. As the scene declined, many of these businesses endured, but became more commercial; that is, they drifted farther and farther away from the anti-materialistic, unconventional patterns of the early hippies. *Rolling Stone*, one of the later underground newspapers to appear, evolved from a loosely organized hippie enterprise to an efficient, highly successful, nationally recognized weekly. "Glitter rock," whose stars are excessively commercial, emerged from acid rock. For all practical intents and purposes, the people involved in these highly successful commercial ventures have been absorbed back into the conventional society.

Many more hippies became involved in the arts and crafts business, which by 1972 supported hundreds in a manner which permitted them to maintain many of the essential patterns of the hippie scene. This commercial enterprise took shape from ragged beginnings. During expansion, many hippies tried to produce art and craft items. At first they lacked basic craft skills, and they emphasized spontaneous expression to such a degree that their products were crude, amateurish, and not highly salable. However, the quality of the crafts improved after several years of practice, on the farms in Mendocino or in industrial warehouses in San Francisco which had been converted by several hippie-commune-businesses—such as, "Project One," "Project Artaud," and "Zeus"—into a cluster of small living and working spaces. They began to successfully market their "roach" clips, sand candles, belts, jackets, dresses, shirts, necklaces, bracelets, rings, hairpieces, pots, lamps, tables, and other items. Either they sold these items to the "head" shops (stores which carried hippie paraphernalia), to other hippie merchants, or directly to customers, usually on stands they set up on the streets or in the flea markets of San Francisco and Berkeley. After several years of skirmishing with city administrations, the hippie merchants were given several locations—San Francisco's Union Square, Ghirardelli Square, the Embarcadero

158

Plaza, and Berkeley's Telegraph Avenue. Sherri Cavan supplies us with a description of the street markets.

> The walkway between Ghirardelli and the Cannery is a solid line of peddlers, with their wares spread out in front of them. Some are alone; others are in groups of the same sex, of mixed sex, with small children, with dogs. There are also musicians and mimes.

> Through the afternoon, crowds of people streamed by. Some were young, some old. Some looked relatively affluent, others seemed rather impoverished. Two women stopped at the woodcarver's stall. They said they were welfare mothers, in town for a convention, to lobby for child care centers. I would have taken them for secretaries, except for the roughness of their hands.

> As people strolled by, they would stop to look at the peddlers' wares; listen to the music, watch the mime. Some took photographs; others engaged the sellers in conversation.

> Among the sellers there was a lively discourse. Through the course of the day, peddlers, in adjacent stalls would chat with one another, examine each other's merchandise, tend one another's stalls. Peddlers from different stalls would wander through the market, chat with others they knew, compare business and prices [*Urban Life*, 1972, pp. 216-217].

DIEHARDS

Surfing. Not all surfers defected, accommodated to conventional society, or went professional. A relatively large number, perhaps thousands, of the old-time surfers ("senile surf freaks") and new recruits tried to carry on the early tradition. Many pockets of these diehards were faraway from Southern California, in places to which surfers fled and locals joined them to preserve the scene. For instance, Northern California, the East Coast, the "Islands" (the Hawaiian Islands)—particularly the other islands, such as Maui and Kauai—New Zealand, Australia, Africa, and France are locations of these pockets.

There has even been one period of revitalization—a neoclassical phase—during which some of the old excitement and vitality came back. This was between 1968 and 1970, when a drastic change in surfboard designed pumped new life into the stagnating sport (as the first real change in surfboard design had contributed so strongly to the articulation of the scene). The boards shrank from an average of 9-½ feet to about 6, and were available in many new designs. This, of course, introduced radical changes in wave riding. "Total involvement," which entailed riding much closer to the broken part of the wave, staying around the "white water," and executing more rapid, frequent, and radical turns, replaced "nose riding" and "trimming," the two main techniques used with the larger boards. The notion of total involvement flowed up on the shore and, in general, there was a renewed commitment to a total, "natural" lifestyle on the beach. In this revitalized period, many artifacts were borrowed from the neighboring hippie scene, particularly drugs and natural foods.

There will probably be hundreds of diehards who will continue the struggle to preserve aspects of the Golden Age of surfing. Perhaps from time to time there will be further revitalizations, which will draw new members who will help recapture the surfing's early excitement.

Hippies. Thousands of hippies continue to follow the old patterns, but, as in surfing, this is done in many distant outposts. Moreover, various offshoots of the hippie scene help preserve much of the earlier style. For instance, in 1973, there were several hundred youths living in Yosemite Park, sleeping in lightweight nylon tents and sharing community kitchens set up in the all-year campground. The youths worked intermittently in the tourist businesses in the park, or returned to the city for unemployment or welfare checks, or for short periods of work. They shared their resources and cooperated with the park rangers by voluntarily cleaning up the park. In return, they were allowed to remain beyond the prescribed limit. Many of them were engaged in rock climbing, and others just enjoyed the beauty, the companionship of other hippies, and the outdoor "natural" life. I would guess there were probably many similar "mutant" offshoots of the hippie scene.

RESIDUES

In addition to enduring in a state of stagnation, these scenes have had a general impact on the larger society. In the case of surfing, there are only a few important residues which will probably never disappear. The sport of wave riding has been developed to a high level of complexity and beauty. Many non-wave-riding patterns diffused out into other social worlds. The surfer's long hair apparently influenced the hippie scene. Likewise, acid rock was at least partly fashioned on surfing music. And the casual dress, nomadism, and anti-employment patterns of surfing floated into the hippie world. But residues of surfing drifted into broader areas of life in America and other parts of the world in many less identifiable ways, such as a generally enhanced appreciation for alternative lifestyles.

The impact of the hippie scene on the society was much more dramatic. The patterns of dress, grooming, speech, art, and music permeated most parts of the society—particularly the exclusive upper layers. Long hair on men, for instance, became the preferred style not only of jocks, but of Wall Street lawyers. By 1973, blue denim was the fashionable cloth of the chic set of New York. And almost everyone listened and danced to rock music. But the impact was more profound than just an imitation of hippie patterns. The scene cleaved through society in a way which might remain for many years. This cleavage was between those persons who became generally sympathetic to the values and the lifestyle (whether or not they actually participated in any of the activities), and those who were antagonistic toward them. This polarization is captured somewhat in the distinction between hip and straight.

Hip people were sympathetic to hippies and tolerant of deviance in general. Moreover, they tended to be politically radical—or at least liberal. Finally, they either used marijuana or did not object to its use. They also may have dressed in some way which reflected their "hipness," but this was not as important as the other attributes. Nor was it necessary that they joined bohemian or other deviant worlds. Straights, on the other hand, were intolerant of hippies and other deviants, and tended to be politically conservative. They, in fact, became so alarmed at the rise of the "counter culture" that they supported a law and order drive aimed at controlling this new threat to their values and institutions, and called up Richard Nixon to restore order. This cleavage has often been mistaken for a "generation gap," because the hippie scene spread first among the young. But the major polariation was not essentially one of age, but one of hipness or straightness, and this polarization was produced more by the hippie move-ment than by any other cause.[8]

We do not want to make the common mistake of extrapolating present trends too far into the future. It is inevitable that other currents will flow over the social terrain, fill the gap between the two sides, and carve new cleavages. The distinctions between hip and straight have already been considerably blurred. But there is no risk in stating that the hippie scene's impact on the American society has been garantuan.

CONCLUSION

It is not clear if another Grand Scene will rise in the near future. Perhaps the social relationships and forces which permitted and fostered these two scenes are disappearing. At present, there are strong indications that we are passing out of relative affluence and into a time of scarcity. If this is true, it is not likely that the society can afford or will tolerate large segments openly—in fact, ostentatiously—avoiding productive careers and spending their entire days doing such things as riding waves, waiting for the surf to come up, tripping out on marijuana, LSD, or some other drug, and thumbing their noses at conventional life. Scenes of this type may be suppressed by collective reactions, or structural impossibilities (e.g., the lack of minimum resources to sustain a leisure lifestyle for large numbers of individuals).

Or perhaps another Grand Scene cannot appear because we have become overly sensitive to it—some degree of inexperience may be necessary for such a scene to develop. Maybe it is like a confidence game, which requires unsuspecting, uninitiated victims. Once you have been taken the game or know about it, you cannot be sucked in. Maybe we have become too "hip," too blasé, too cynical, to allow ourselves to participate in a social experiment with the intensity that an incipient scene must generate.

However—maybe not. Maybe we are in a lull between Grand Scenes.[9]

5 | SETTING the STAGE

Having examined types of scenes and their content, we can now turn to a more thorough analysis of the social processes which (stretching the metaphor to its breaking point) "set the stage" for these scenes. We will look at these processes in two separate ways—"materially" and "ideally." These have often been presented separately—in fact, counterposed—as explanations for social phenomena. I will not argue for one or the other, but will use both, particularly since the factors in which we are most interested seem to have been influenced by distinct processes which neatly divide into one type or the other. We will start with an examination of the social structure changes (materialism) which pried people loose from their provincial traditional institutions and cultures and left them with more free time and money, but without the traditional foundations of meaning and purpose, nor a "community" to supply human contact. Then we will turn to the development of the idea of the "actor" and of life as a drama (idealism) which equiped people with a "dramaturgic" mentality.

The social-structural changes we will examine are those which have been sociology's center of attention during most of its short life span (which, not accidentally, corresponds almost exactly to the hundred fifty years of changes brought on by the industrial revolution). These changes—industrializa-

163

tion, urbanization, and bureaucratization, which will be referred to collectively as *modernization*—are probably
familiar, and my comments on them will be brief. Then we
shall look more closely at the latter part of the industrial
revolution, during which different conditions produced new
social circumstances and responses. We will call this second
era *relativization*, and it will not be as familiar as modernization was.

MODERNIZATION: STAGE ONE

Industrialization has moved the vast majority of the
population of industrial nations into a nonpropertied, sala-
ried, economically and politically subordinate position to
business organizations or government bureaucracies. In most
cases, the "masses" have merely shifted from one type of
subordination to another. Nonetheless, in capitalistic, industrial nations—and it is a capitalistic nation on which we are
focused—it has resulted in frequent economic dislocations.
Consequently, large-or small-scale layoffs and other termi-
naltions of employment occur whenever economic exigencies
dictate. What this means for modern employees is that,
besides enduring periods of unemployment, often they must
seek new employment of the same or different type, relocate
geographically to seek new employment, and sometimes
switch careers, even relatively late in life.

Another consequence of shifting most persons to this
productive mode is that the number of hours spent in
"production" has been reduced. In this century, in the
United States, the work week was shortened from 69.7 hours
in 1850 to 38.5 hours in 1960.[1]

In addition to reducing the working hours, if we can
ignore recessions and depressions (and also ignore the fantas-
tically lethal wars which have followed the industrial revolution—admittedly, not easy), the industrial revolution has
simplified the problem of *physical* survival. In the contemporary society, particularly in the United States, survival has

been reduced to "making a living"—a very difficult act for many who are unfavorably located in the stratified, economic world. However, compared to the survival problems which beset populations in earlier periods, it is a significant reduction. Now instead of having to worry about blizzards, drought, floods, plagues, marauding bands, excessively rapacious, onerous, and capricious totalitarian despots and their kin, and many other variable and dangerous forces which persistently or occasionally threatened life, most persons merely have to hold a job, rent an apartment, buy a car and a few clothes, and they survive.[2]

Besides simplifying the struggle for survival, the industrial revolution has filled the space of modern citizens' lives with an endless variety of mechanical devices which impinge upon their daily routines in many different and important ways. Two important categories of these mechanical devices are those which have increased people's mobility at least a thousandfold and others which have deluged them with a flood of information about the world. The ramifications of these machines will be explored in our later discussion of relativization.

Big cities emerged along with modern industry, but, more important, a new *urban* society developed concurrently. With the development of modern transportation and communication systems—subways, trains, cars, airplanes, trucks, super-highways, bridges, elevators, high rises, radios, television sets, and movies—not only can and do most people in modern societies live crammed in large, dense cities or in the suburban sprawl around their centers, but even those people outside these rings are drawn into the urban sphere by tie lines of modern communication and merchandising.[3]

In the big cities (and they are the vortex of the new theatrical dynamic), a new urbanized life emerged. In this new life, people live among and commingle with each other, get around and away from each other, and still keep private many of the areas of their lives which used to be public.

Bureaucratization. Also developing along with modern industry was a hierarchical style of social organization, the bureaucracy, which made the industrial society possible. Most modern people are attached in some direct way to this type of organization and all live in a world which has been profoundly altered by it. Its primary characteristic is specialization of work. Jobs are arranged in a stack, with each level having authority over some positions below, and being responsible to some positions above. A second fundamental characteristic is that jobs exist separately from the people occupying them. In other words, the qualities of individuals selected to fill jobs are subordinated to the characteristics of bureaucratic positions. The duties, rights, and definitions of the positions have been established to further the goals of the organization and not to satisfy individual needs or desires.

Bureaucratization means that modern citizens find themselves doing very specialized work, occupying a niche in which their duties and rights as part of the bureaucracy are much more important than their unique, or idiosyncratic characteristics.[4]

THE INDIVIDUAL IN THE MODERN CITY

The changes which modernization produced in the life routine and psychology of the modern urbanite have probably been discussed more than any other set of issues in sociology. Most of the commentary and theorizing generally agrees that life in the city has become more impersonal, specialized, and compartmentalized. Alvin Toffler offers one of the better discriptions of this new urban mode.

> Rather than entangling ourselves with the whole man, we plug into a module of his personality. Each personality can be imagined as a unique configuration of thousands of such modules. Thus, no whole person is interchangeable with any other. But certain modules are. Since we are seeking only to buy a pair of shoes and not the friendship, love or hate of the salesman, it is not necessary for us to tap into or engage with all the other

modules that form his personality. Our relationship is safely limited. There is limited liability on both sides. The relationship entails certain accepted forms of behavior and communication. Both sides understand, consciously or otherwise, the limitations and laws. Difficulties arise only when one or another party oversteps the tacitly understood limits, when he attempts to connect up with some module not relevant to the function at hand [p. 97].

This means that we generally relate to each other with much less emotion and on a very narrow range of issues, concerns, or tasks; and that we keep most of our personal lives out of our day-to-day contacts. In a sense, the relationship between the clerk and the customer is an extreme of the narrow, depersonalized, compartmentalized interactional mode which is more or less typical of the modern city.

A salient psychological side effect of this new interactional mode is that individuals have had wedges of doubt driven between what they do and who they are. They carry on the limited tasks of their jobs in modern organizations or interact in a very narrow manner with most people they meet, while knowing that they are in no way uniquely meaningful in either circumstance. This knowledge inevitably gives them the sense that the "roles" they perform are artificial and separate from their real selves.

The industrialized system of production of goods and the capitalistic system of ownership then have psychologically separated many or most workers from their work. For employees, work has lost its essential meaning—that of being humans' cooperative effort to maintain their lives (or some niche) on earth. Thus, coupled with frequent economic dislocations, work has ceased to be fundamental to the meaning worlds out of which many individuals construct their adult identifies, their career plans, and their social positions. In addition, hope of promotions, knowledge of transfers, or fear of layoffs or firings orient workers to future states of being which further loosen their attachment to work. People seek jobs more often for money and benefits such as short hours, vacations, travel, or other more vague dimensions, like "excitement", instead of as a primary source of meaning, identity, and status.

The final important aspect of the change in individual conditions because of modernization, is that most people have become freer. The first way freedom has expanded is in social mobility. Modernization has tumbled or rearranged structures of caste and class and traditional institutions to make room for new industrial and urban forms. Consequently, people can participate in many social institutions which were formerly closed to them, and they are no longer forced to participate in others (such as religious institutions) which used to be obligatory. In addition, modern people have increased physical mobility. The proliferation of automobiles, air travel, and the like, the increased affluence of the average person—making pulling up stakes and moving, or taking time off and traveling, possible—and the removal of political and social restrictions on travel have opened up the world to modern urbanite, who has taken advantage of this freedom and moved around the globe at an astonishing rate.

MODERNIZATION: STAGE TWO

After World War II, which is a convenient and probably a natural reference point, the industrial revolution entered a new phase. New forms of technology, particularly in communications and transportation, were developed, and the United States and other industrial nations reached new heights of material opulence. The social structure was further rearranged, and the citizens of modern nations became more nearly cultural relativists.

These structural rearrangements, outgrowths of modernization, promoted cultural relativism by setting off an explosive expansion of general knowledge and experience, that weakened or broke the connections most people had had with local sacred institutions and culture, (at least with those aspects which had survived the first stage of the industrial revolution). The importance of this cultural relativism to the growth of scenes is such that we will now explore some of the factors that caused it.

Moving Around. As mentioned above, modernization freed people to move both temporarily and permanently more frequently or easily than they had previously been able to. After World War II, the rapid movement of Americans from place to place increased steadily. In fact, the war itself first set the nation in motion because so many people moved to cities from rural communities or other areas to take part in war-related industries. Large numbers also moved around the country or the world as members of the armed forces, or in related capacities.

After the war and a brief period of respite, the motion began again. Increases in affluence and transportation, the rapid growth or relocation of industrial organizations, shifts in employment (and unemployment) patterns, and the continuing interest in new places which had been generated by the war all accelerated geographical mobility to a blur.

A few indicators of the increases in mobility are useful to convey a sense of its relative increases. Buckminster Fuller has calculated that, in 1914, the typical American traveled about 340 miles a year with the aid of a horse and all existing mechanical means. In contrast, contemporary Americans travel in excess of 12,000 miles a year in their cars alone. In the late 1960s, 4 million Americans a year traveled to Europe. Since World War II approximately one-fifth of the population change residences at least once a year, a 50 percent increase from the 1935 to 1940 period. There is growing evidence that in the decades before 1920, even back to the civil war, Americans changed residences as often or more often than we do today. However, Claude Fischer and Ann Stueve argue (*New Society,* November 1976) that most of the earlier movers were working class and after 1920 middle class. I deduce from this and other historical indicators that the earlier movers stayed in familiar social worlds by moving to other parts of the city to join other members of their family, class, or ethnic group, or migrated with a familiar cohort. Modern movers are more often young, middle class and leave home to take up residence among unfamiliar people.

We want to stress here that one of the major consequences of the supercharged mobility has been that relatively narrow, ethnocentric compartments into which most Americans previously fit have been perforated or torn down. Moving from place to place and changing one set of friends for another, have expanded the contacts which people have with varied social worlds.

The Media. Perhaps even more important than increased mobility in expanding the knowledge and experience available to modern citizens has been the postwar media, particularly television. Since the war, virtually everyone in the United States has had their world drastically altered by this pervasive electronic medium. Every home, neighborhood, nook, and hollow of America has been flooded by a torrent of information about an endless variety of subjects. Many critics have argued that this stream pouring over Americans from the "boob tube" has been mostly glop which nurtures an unsophisticated, mythical, conformity-encouraging version of life. I strongly believe that such criticism misses the point and, in fact, reflects a righteous intellectual snobbishness. Instead, I would argue that, considering the original level of knowledge or experience of the majority of the population, much of the content of television has been fresh and strange from the outset, and its long-term effect has been to steadily broaden most people's intellectual horizons.

We must regard the radio as the first disseminator of information on a massive national scale. But TV has imparted much more information about a lot of previously unfamiliar facets of living on earth (and its moon) to the average citizen.

Thus, this generation's geometric rise in information began with television news programs, documentaries, special reports, special features, and regular programming—all of which have continually widened in scope and sophistication.

In addition, TV has promoted a *broader national perspective* on political and social issues and on life in general. It is true that the bulk of TV programming could be called bland, even in the early years, but there has always been some spicy stuff sprinkled in with the pap—e.g., Omnibus, Playhouse 90, GE Television Theatre, and the other live dramas written by such talented people as Paddy Chayevsky, Reginald Rose, and Rod Serling. As television developed, an increasing percentage of its programming has been delivered from a relatively intelligent perspective. Remember that "All in the Family" replaced "Bonanza" as the most popular show on TV, and in terms of consciousness expansion, "All in the Family" is light years away from earlier television situation comedy series (though of course still frighteningly bland when compared to the British series from which it was adapted, "Till Death Do Us Part").

Finally, television has had a broadening impact on the knowledge and perspective of its audience by conveying a singularly immediate experience of the subject matter it treats. Through newscasting, documentaries, special programs and quality drama, relatively full-dimensioned chunks of real life from unfamiliar parts or strange lands are plunked down into the middle of the livingroom. When done well—e.g., "Roots," a television phenomenon in 1977—television provides an effect far closer to first-hand experience than can the written word, and thus is a stronger promoter of understanding, identification and empathy.

It may still be argued that network television, instead of being broadening, has narrowed the perspective of Americans since most of its content has been slanted toward a white, middle-class, consumer-oriented presentation of American life. It is certainly true—particularly in the early years and particularly in the "sitcom" family shows—that television bombarded people with an "idealized" conception of an American life from which many, perhaps most, Americans have departed. While this may have had the effect of homogenizing the culture by breaking down the barriers between variant subcultures, it may also have had the effect of cutting people loose from their own subcultures. More recently, television has been presenting many variants from the middle-class white family theme—e.g., *Sanford and Son*. TV's long-term impact has been to introduce viewers to different life-styles and perspectives, and simultaneously to loosened them from their former sacred, taken-for-granted beliefs and values.

Other facets of the media—most notably, periodicals—have also contributed to the expansion of the ordinary citizen's vistas. Since World War II, not only has there been a steady increase in the information about the world in all magazines (and newspapers, for that matter), but there has been a steady increase of magazines dealing with specialized subjects. The change in the offerings on the typical magazine rack in the drug, tobacco, or bookstore from about 1940 to 1970 is almost unbelievable. Formerly the rack would have been limited to the old, reliable, general issue magazines, such as *Saturday Evening Post, Collier's, Liberty, Life, Look, Time,* and *Newsweek,* and perhaps a few aimed at a special audience—such as *Ladies' Home Journal, Scientific American, Popular Mechanics*, and *Movie Screen*. A good sized rack today has literally hundreds of different magazines dealing with everything from dune buggies to magic. The general drift has been away from "general" to specialized magazines. *Saturday Evening Post, Collier's, Liberty, Life*, and *Look* have either disappeared completely or are attempting to make comebacks with revised formats. The proliferation of specialty magazines has been amazing. Every sport, hobby, interest, major city, or profession has its own magazine or magazines. In fact, the contemporary magazine rack is a buffet of variant lifestyles.

The growth of the book publishing business and particularly the appearance of the mass paperback has also contributed significantly to the knowledge explosion. The majority of paperbacks sold since their appearance have been fiction (and a lot of it trashy fiction, at that), but the number of quality novels, classics included, which have reached every level of the society by way of the paperback has been tremendous. Moreover, the American public has been offered, and has accepted, a steady stream of popularized scientific and social scientific works. For instance, David Riesman's *The Lonely Crowd*; William Whyte's *Organization Man*; Rachel Carson's *Silent Spring*; Charles Reich's *The Greening of America*; and Alvin Toffler's *Future Shock*, in their period of heavy sales, were available in most stores with a sizable collection of paperbacks, are still available in some stores, and collectively, have sold millions of copies.

These books did more than simply assist in the expansion of knowledge and experience, they added another dimension to it. The concepts, ideas, and perspectives developing in formerly isolated and exclusive scientific or academic spheres were rapidly broadcast, though in simplified forms, to the general public. Consequently, the "folk" mentality in the postwar period has not lagged far behind expert or scientific perspectives. Today, ideas from the loftier reaches of the intelligentsia gravitate quickly down to the interested lay person.

College Education. In 1900, there was one college degree granted for every 2,000 people living in the United States. According to the U.S. Census Bureau, by 1957, this had increased to one for every 420 and by 1970, to one for every 180. In 1956, twenty percent of the youth between 18 and 21 were enrolled in college; in 1970, the figure was thirty five percent.

We must point out that college education is not just an extension of high school. In a way very relevant for our discussion, it is qualitatively different. High school has been an enterprise of teaching the basic skills—"reading, 'riting, and 'rithmetic"—*and* of inculcating the student into the official American culture. History, literature, civics, social studies courses, and many regular school routines, such as saluting the flag, have been carefully structured with the intention of developing respect for the country's major institutions and of imparting a restained, self-congratulatory, status-quo-oriented perspective on the country's history and present relationships. Very conservative and moralistic guardians have watched over the high school with a piercing eye, which is the reason we hear so often of "controversial" history books being rejected by high school administrations, or "radical" English teachers being fired by school boards of small communities because they assigned some "subversive" or "dirty" book like *Soul on Ice.*[5] Generally, the fight for control over the high school by more conservative interest groups in the society has been intense.

In college, on the other hand, the thrust—at least in the humanities and social sciences—in most good liberal arts schools has been toward promoting a critical, relativistic, even iconoclastic perspective on the society's history, institutions, and present internal and external relationships. A "good" liberal college education has been one which taught people to think critically. To a great extent, this means that they have learned to stand back from all they learned previously and to view their former assumptions from a more impartial and rational viewpoint. The effect of this perspective was to undermine one's beliefs and strong commitments to one's institutions. Ronald Reagan, Governor of California from 1968 to 1976, was getting at the truth when, in 1970, after years of campus "radicalism" in California, he publically identified the professors in the state colleges and universities as the culprits who were spreading the radical, non-conformist, relativisitic perspective among wave after wave of college students. The real blame (or credit) does not go to the professors, however, but to the general momentum of a liberal arts education.[6]

Modernization lifted most Americans from small, rural, totally involved social worlds and put them into busy cities and an impersonal, specialized, and emotionally neutral social life. The technological and social developments after World War II wrenched them loose from their sacred institutions and the culture on which they rested. In these ways, the industrial revolution first germinated and then accomplished a rather extensive social and cultural dislocation.

Cultural dislocation is a side product of the acquisition of a culturally relativistic perspective. To understand fully what this latter means, we must look at the converse—cultural *ethnocentricity*. In most places, in most times in the span of human history, humans have grown up in societies which equipped them with full-blown self contained systems of beliefs, values, and symbols giving cognitive meaning, moral justification, and mystical value to their lives, and the events around them. These systems of beliefs, values, symbols, and meanings are part of a particular culture, and it is essential to remember that members of a particular culture tend to consider theirs the *only* culture. They consider their culture the only way to live and see things, and all other systems as inferior, immoral, or nonhuman. This view is called ethnocentricity. One of the universal processes which gives a culture this lofty and exclusive status is religion. A culture becomes inextricably tied to superhuman, godly forces, and the patterns of the society and, in fact, the society itself is infused with profound, mystical qualities.

The tendency to create and maintain such a culture is inherent in the social process. A gang, a high school clique, a fraternity, a corporation, or a nation, as long as they exist as viable groups or collectivities, will tend to develop a set of unique values, beliefs, and symbols which give meaning, moral weight, even mystical value, to their activities and their social group.

However, to maintain an *ethnocentric* culture, the group or collectivity must keep itself protected from other contradictory systems of meaning which undermine, corrode, and loosen commitment to it. Extreme physical isolation or discrimination accomplished this in earlier periods of human history. Some cultures have struggled tenaciously to be separate and ethnocentric long after physical isolation from other cultures ceases.[7]

Other groups have been able to maintain enough isolation, though they are in close contact with other, "dominant" cultures by controlling education and other processes of inculcation into the culture until people have thoroughly "internalized" the patterns of the "minority" culture. If there is considerable contact between adults of different cultural groups, there must be a heavy emphasis in the cultural definitions of the minority group regarding the reasons the minority culture is superior, and the reasons why people who do not follow that culture are wrong—e.g. their being under the influence of the devil. The gypsies are a good example of a people who have lived in European and American societies for centuries yet have been able to a remarkable degree to preserve their distinct culture. They have accomplished this largely by carefully controlling the socialization of their children, who are kept out of the host society's schools.[8]

However, these extreme examples are rare, and the mechanisms for maintaining isolation and exclusion have limits. When too much contradictory material bombards individuals, particularly when they are young, then unless their commitment to the culture is intense, belief in the culture is necessarily weakened. The culture seems demystified, and all values become somewhat relative.[9]

This is exactly what has occurred in the United States since World War II. Several factors have destroyed or seriously damaged the physical, cognitive, moral, and mystical separations between the cultures within our society: (1) the mobility patterns, which greatly increased the physical contact between disparate people; (2) the media, which in their cumbersome, but relentless manner broadened the experiences and increased the knowledge people had about others, other places, and other things; (3) the paperbacks, which added to the knowledge explosion and gave it more perspective; and (4) mass college education, which more directly encouraged cultural relativism. In the process of losing their hold on their disparate cultures, individuals have become aware of, able to understand, and appreciative of other "subcultures" within their urban world. In other words, they have become subcultural relativists.

Though we want to emphasize that many perhaps most urbanites' relationships to their culture has been altered drastically, we do not want to suggest that entire cultures have disintegrated. Even for those whose culture has been demystified, there remains a fat layer of cultural "stuff" which serves as insulation between them and social disorder. This layer contains the innumerable ordinary, everyday definitions of objects and transactions which are never considered "consciously." These are definitions regarding passing on the street, eating, going to the toilet, entering a room, and an infinite number of other social maneuvers which individuals accomplish by dipping down into a "taken-for-granted" repertoire of maneuvers and interpretations. Unless questioned by contradictory patterns, these continue to be put into service "unthinkingly," and in this way the cultural process continues to equip us to handle many of our everyday transactions with ease. It is the more explicit and more general values and beliefs and the institutions built on them which have been challenged in the increased contacts between diverse cultural systems and which have been thusly demystified.

FREEDOM AND ALIENATION

What have been the consequences of the demystification of the culture? Have the severed ties brought freedom or alienation? On the one hand, when relationships to the society's institutions are no longer obligatory or infused with mystical meanings, individuals can consider and choose a greater range of life alternatives. They may choose to marry or not, choose from a broader range of people, aspire to a great variety of occupations, and embark on formerly unacceptable lifestyles. Presently, when they depart from the old ways the most serious sanction they experience is usually some flak from parents. Since the family has also been demystified, the parents' ire is no longer frightening or potent. So, during the 1960s, droves of "high-class" sorority girls became involved in radical student demonstrations, "clean-cut jocks" grew shoulder-length hair, and "nice" Jewish girls made it with black men (and a few even built bombs in cellars).

On the other hand, however, the demystification has liberated individuals from institutional affiliations which used to infuse their lives with purpose, meaning, and activities. Some have rebounded and re-embraced older sacred institutions (like Buddhism) or newer mystical movements, like the Moon cult. These attempts can only be partially successful, because once demystification has occurred it is difficult to reinvest any part of society with import or mystical meaning. In the past, overriding national purpose such as a popular war took up the slack and involved smaller segments of the potentionally disaffliated.[10] The Vietnam war failed to do this because of widespread disagreement over its morality and legitimacy. Since 1950, no national or society-wide systems of purpose or meaning have appeared to fill the vacancies in the lives of the liberated. Consequently, large segments of urban populations are socially and psychologically available for new forms of social interaction and for participation in new social worlds.

THE UNCOMMITTED

The disaffiliated break naturally into two categories relative to their degree of liberation or alienation, and their degree of participation in traditional social forms. In the first category are the institutionally uncommitted, those who continue to participate in a minimal fashion in many of the society's conventional social organizations. They hold a job, which is a necessity for most people, and beyond this they marry and have children. They may have a few friends whom they meet at work or in their neighborhood and with whom they occasionally pass leisure hours. Less often, they keep up some irregular contact with their nuclear family—their parents and siblings—and their extended family—their uncles, aunts, and cousins. They seldom participate in any formal or informal social groups, such as church groups, political organizations, or social clubs. Scott Greer summarizes several studies of the patterns of participation of modern urbanites, with the following conclusion:

> The picture that emerges is of a society in which the conjugal family is extremely powerful among all types of population. This small, primary group structure is one basic area of involvement; at the other pole is work, a massive absorber of time, but an activity that is rarely related to the family through "outside" friendship with on-the-job associates. Instead, the family, its kin, and its friendship group, is relatively free-floating, within the world of large-scale secondary associations. Burgess has pointed out that the weakening of a primary community results in the increasing relative dependence of individuals upon the conjugal family as a source of primary relationships; this same principle explains the persisting importance of extended kin and the proliferation of close friendships in urban America. In the metropolis the community as a solid phalanx of friends or acquaintances does not exist; if individuals are to have a community in the older sense of communion, they must make it for themselves. These conditions are at an extreme in the highly urban neighborhoods, and there friendships and kinship are, relatively, most important in the average individual's social world. In other kinds of neighborhoods the family is usually identified, although weakly, with the local community; it "neighbors," but strictly within bounds. By and large, the conjugal family group keeps itself to itself; outside is the world—formal organization, work, and the communities [pp. 93-94].

At present, most of the institutionally uncommitted do not possess a strong commitment to any set of general or universal values or beliefs, conventional or unconventional, nor a consuming dedication to national or general societal goals. Someone registers as a Democrat, but votes for a Republican, perhaps because he likes a particular issue. Or, increasingly, he does not vote at all. He has no trust in the government, business, the schools, or any other large societal institutions. He cares more about "crime in the streets," the fuel shortage, city employee strikes, or other things which affect him directly and materially, than he does about the quality of the environment, human rights, the world starvation problem, or other global or national problems.

Some of the members of this growing segment in the United States and other modern industrial nations are relatively unattached to traditional institutions and the society's formal social organizations, but are searching for locations where they can tie into networks of other persons, engage in collective activities, and find new sources for an overall life design. Their material opulence and condition of demystification or relativism turn them away from instrumental or task-oriented activities and toward expressive, collective forms. The reappearance of an overriding national purpose, or "hard times," may reorient them to work and the country, but in the meantime the uncommitted are free and disposed to perform in the activity systems and lifestyle scenes which were described in the preceding chapters.

BOHEMIANS, RADICALS, AND OTHER OUTSIDERS

On the fringes of modern society is a growing number of more completely disaffiliated. These persons—the bohemians, the radicals, or others who have made a more complete break with the conventional society—are active in constructing and experimenting with life in alternative ways. They participate in conventional realms only to the degree necessary to sustain life or stay out of jail—but not always the latter (or at times, the former, for that matter). In fact, it was the members of this category who in the 1950s and 1960s participated vigorously in the activity systems and alternative lifestyles which were widely publicized and who, thereby, opened the gates for mass entrance into the new expressive scenes.

Before we describe the growth of the idea of life as drama, we must explore a process fundamental to general development of ideas. Ideas, new or old, can be described as "metaphors." If we trace the meaning of our concepts as they appear in language (and we must keep in mind that language is more than just the vehicle of ideas; it may be their very substance), we see that new understandings or meanings are developed when a term applied in one place is applied to new, different, situations. Thus, existing understandings are borrowed for new phenomena; then experiences with the new phenomena accrue to the metaphor, and its original use is lost. For instance, let's take the first paragraph in a story on the first page of the April 2, 1974, *New York Times.*

Leaders of municipal labor unions called yesterday for cost-of-living raises for their members similar to those won by the transit workers.

With a dictionary, it is possible to follow the metaphorical process back at least one step for many of the concepts. In the above usage, the word *leaders* derives from the Anglo-Saxon word "to go" and brings to its new application the connotation of those who proceed. *Union* derives from the Latin word for a single, large pearl. *Raises* is again a physical motion concept translated to nonphysical relationships. *Member* used to refer to a part of the body. And so on. We could continue through the paragraph, down the page, and eventually find all the metaphorical roots of all the words. The point is that borrowing understandings from one object, relationship, or activity and applying them to another, perhaps newer, phenomenon is how ideas grow. We shall argue that this is what occurred when humans borrowed the drama to help understand social life. But it not only led to a different understanding of life, it changed life. In the manner in which ideas structure reality, life became more like the theatre.

The emergence of a theatrical mentality is important to an understanding of the development of the age of scenes. People do not experience others, themselves, or the world as these things "are," but filtered through individual ideas or perspectives. Moreover, people's ideas are not simply the products of social structure nor of individual invention. Ideas grow according to their own social processes and then play a role in structuring situations. The idea or perspective that life is like the theatre had its own development and then spread among the disaffiliated, fully equipping them for their performances in modern, dramatic urban life.

The idea that life is like the drama developed almost simultaneously with the drama itself. Starting in the fifth century, "Periclean" Greece, after written drama (with actors and a stage) had evolved, many people made references to life as drama. Plato is the source of several of these—for instance, as in *Philebus*, where he wrote of "the great stage of human life." In the *Laws*, he employed the imagery of a puppet show in which people are puppets, manipulated by the gods. The cave metaphor in *The Republic* is a related system of ideas. Much later, an Alexandrian Greek poet, Palladus, used the dramatic metaphor more completely:

All life is a stage and a play
Either learn to play, laying
   your gravity aside
Or bear with life's pains

Wherever there has been a highly developed theatre, and, therefore, one in which people show intense interest, there has been the recognition that not only is the play an explicit representation of life, but that it also has implicit connotations of life. Many, particularly the successful, dramatists—playwrights, actors, directors, and the like—need exceptional insight into the interactional processes of human life as well as a great deal of understanding and knowledge of the salient themes, events, and issues of their times. In a sense, the dramatists were psychologists and sociologists long before these professions became institutionalized.

Consequently, whenever there is an active period in the theatre dramatists and their colleagues explicitly make the other potentional comparison between life and the theatre—that, as the play is like life, life is like the play. For instance, in Spain during the sixteenth century (a high point in the history of the theatre) the use of the metaphor was so widespread that it led Cervantes to have Sancho Panza remark to Don Quixote's use of the life/stage comparison: "A fine comparison, although not so new that I haven't heard it on various occasions before—like the one of the game of chess."

In the great period of drama, Elizabethan England, the use of the metaphor is abundant. Shakespeare, of course, makes repeated use of it and his famous lines from *As You Like It* stand out as the most complete and developed use in literature:

All the world's a stage,
And all the men and women merely players.
They have their exits and their entrances;
And one man in his time plays many parts. . . .

But many other writers in and around the theatre at that time also compared life to it.[11]

I suppose it is inherent in its nature that drama be employed as a metaphor for life. In attempting to enact life, drama inevitably imitates real life structures with revealing insight into their implicit makeup. So recognition of parallels occurs whenever and wherever there is an intense preoccupation with drama. In the past, the number of people who did the recognizing was limited to dramatists, other "intellectuals," or "men of letters," and the "leisure class," who regularly attended the theatre.[12] The theatrical insight and a resultant more dramatic mentality and interactional mode did not spread out into the general society until much later.

Before the theatrical metaphor reached the masses, however, the social sciences appeared and a new category of specialists—with much less artistic finesse and heavier hands, but with more discipline—started probing into the structure of the "self" and the interrelationships between individuals. They quickly borrowed the existing insights of the dramatists and turned to the theatre as a source of more. Theory construction was their main concern, and they worked more systematically and thoroughly on the theatrical methaphor. They developed it as an "analytical" tool—that is, as a theoretical device to understand concrete behavior, but not necessarily to represent it. However, they did this at a time when the theatricality of life was being recognized by more and more lay people. In fact, the social scientists' work, disseminated through the popularizers of scientific works and into the growing numbers of college-educated, contributed to the spread of the view that life is like a theatre. In this way, social scientists were puffing along in front of the pack, both running from and leading it.

Since sociologists developed a more complete and systematic "dramaturgic" model of everyday life, since the growing number of students going to universities had some passing brush with sociology and learned the metaphor life as theatre if nothing else, and since popularizers of sociological theory spread their the theatrical mentality and thereby dramatized everyday life, we shall now trace the emergence of "role theory" in sociology.

THE THEATRE AND SOCIOLOGY

In this century, the imagery of the theatre supplied sociology with some of its core concepts—role, role performance, role definitions, or, in general, "role theory." However, two different images of life as a theatre were embraced by different "schools of thought" in sociology. The first, which traces back to Plato's version of the theatre-life comparison, is that humans are caught in an enterprise in which the parts have been laid out for them, and the drama is written and directed from some location outside their conscious meaning worlds. For Plato, it is the gods who are pulling the strings, manipulating the puppets on life's stage. In system or structural-functional sociology, the stage is set and the play directed by exigencies and unintended consequences of group living. The humans, in both versions, believing that what they do is "real" and important, unthinkingly perform roles which contribute to an enterprise which they do not fully comprehend. It seems only to be the philosophers or the sociologists who can free themselves from the play and recognize life's overall, dramalike nature.

We are more interested here in the second use in sociology which focuses more on the "conscious actor." In this view, life is like the theatre, not so much because humans are locked in a system of roles, but more because, like the actor on the stage, they are aware that they are trying to play out roles in conjunction with each other. This is more like Shakespeare's use of the comparison in which the drama of life is secular, not divine.[13] While interacting, people remain aware of two essential aspects of their involvement in a collective drama: (1) they are more than just their present role, and there are other facets of themselves which they reveal in other settings or keep completely private; (2) they are aware that others are watching their performance, as would an audience.

In this use of the metaphor, the actors may not be fully aware of the overall theatrical quality of life, but they are aware that they are performing roles in front of others and audiences, though they may not even use those terms and, thereby, they do not explicitly use the dramaturgic metaphor. Whereas Plato's version was more like a puppet show, this one is like traditional theatre, in which the actors learn, rehearse, and perform a script, but in doing so remain aware that they are more than the totality of their roles.

The most complete use of this view of life as a theatre in sociology is in the work of Erving Goffman. But there is a long series of insights which builds up to Goffman's expansive, detailed, and profound use of the theatrical viewpoint. Sociology has looked back, gathered those scattered insights, and strung them together into one traditional strand, which has been labelled "symbolic interaction."[14] Max Weber and Georg Simmel supplied the first and most valuable pieces for the strand. Weber, in attempting to explain social order, began his analysis from the subjective viewpoint of the actor.[15] He suggested that humans can understand the behavior of others through a process in which they place themselves in others' social positions. This would allow them—at least in part—to know subjectively what others are thinking and doing. Simmel added to this the important insight that, though people have "social selves" which emerge in their social interactions, there is always a part of themselves which is held back.

In American sociology, another piece for the strand was provided by Charles Horton Cooley, in *Human Nature and the Social Order*, Cooley argued that individuals become social beings, and thereby human beings, in their interaction in primary groups. In this face-to-face cooperative interaction, humans develop characteristics such as kindness, a sense of justice and sociability, and a conception of themselves. The acquisition of both a benevolent human nature *and* a view of self occurs because humans are able to understand to some degree what others are thinking of them, a process of reciprocity which Cooley compared to the looking glass. Through the looking glass of other's minds, people become aware of themselves and adopt a collective consciousness.

W. I. Thomas added the next link with *The Child in America,* which is the definition of the "situation." Thomas recognized that if people believe that something is real, it has real consequences. Therefore, the definition that people impose upon a situation is the essential component of its composition. George Herbert Mead succeeded in stringing the separate pieces together. First, he converted Thomas' definition of the situation into a dynamic, collective process by *Mind, Self, and Society*. With Mead, the definitions which give a situation its reality, as well as the various roles which actors perform in relation to each other, are in a continuous process of construction in ongoing interaction. People interpret the language and gestures of others, put themselves in others' roles, and assume their viewpoints. Thus they are constantly engaged in building and revising a set of meanings about the situation, themselves, and others.

Mead also made important advances in the area of self-conception, which contributes to the dramaturgic imagery. He saw the self as composed of two separate essential parts, which he labelled the *I* and the *Me*. It is the I which, so to speak, is aware of itself and is watching itself perform in actual situations. But it is the Me which, from the vantage point of the I, has objective existence in the world and in situations. In other words, the I views the Me as an object in situations and develops an array of meanings attached to the self as an object. So it is the Me which is the role, and it is the I which is the performer.

One last dramaturgic component from Mead's tremendous contribution was his study of the audience. Individuals, Mead suggests, not only form an abstraction of themselves in situations, but a generalized conception of "others"—the abstracted audience witnessing, evaluating, and judging the performance. This is the omnipresent and slippery "they" of our lives, which Mead calls the "generalized other," and we hold it to be analogous to the audience in the drama of everyday life.

After Mead, the dramaturgic "model" was developed explicitly and forcefully in sociology. As mentioned above, the fullest, richest elaboration was accomplished by Erving Goffman,[16] but others also made direct use of the metaphor. For instance, Kenneth Burke, who was also directly influential to Goffman's work, converted symbolic interaction into an explicitly dramaturgic tradition, and found more than a metaphorical congruence between life and the theatre.[17] But it is Goffman who takes the metaphor, goes out into the world, and produces convincing—but devastatingly cynical and derogatory—analyses of everyday social life.

In the introduction to his first book, *Presentation of Self in Everyday Life*, Goffman establishes the theme which will dominate most of his first *five* books by quoting at length from a novel by William Samson. The following paragraph from the quoted passages is enough to show Goffman's intention:

> But in any case, he [Preedy, an Englishman on a holiday] took care to avoid catching anyone's eye. First of all, he had to make it clear to those potential companions of his holiday that they were of no concern to him whatsoever. He stared through them, round them, over them—eyes lost in space. The beach might have been empty. If by chance a ball was thrown his way, he looked surprised; then let a smile of amusement lighten his face (Kindly Preedy), looked round dazed to see that there *were* people on the beach, tossed it back with a smile to himself and not a smile at the people, and then resumed carelessly his nonchalant survey of space.

In this book, *Presentation of Self in Everyday Life*, and in *Asylums, Encounters, Stigma,* and *Interaction Ritual,* Goffman moves from setting to setting, analyzing social life from the theatrical viewpoint. His model has two basic theatrical themes. The first is that individuals acting in social contexts present and manage impressions of themselves with an awareness that others watch them.

> Sometimes the individual will act in a thoroughly calculating manner, expressing himself in a given way solely in order to give the kind of impression to others that is likely to evoke from them a specific response he is concerned to obtain [p. 67].

The other is that individuals, while knowingly presenting a self in front of audiences, remain aware that they have an existence separate from the overt, ongoing action in the social setting. Goffman deals explicitly with this latter theme in his essay "Role Distance" in *Encounters*. In some of his essays, such as several in *Asylums*, he focuses on the relationship between the presented self and the inner self.

These two themes, which stemmed directly from the symbolic interaction tradition traced above, are openly theatrical. Moreover, Goffman turns to the theatre time and again for more material to fill out the theatre life comparison. For instance, his various analyses include concepts such as, "front stage," "backstage," "performers," "audiences," "role distance," "role segregation," and "audience segregation." In some essays or chapters in these five books, he shifts to the related metaphor of the game. But the imagery is the same; actors performing self-consciously in an enterprise which they are explicitly aware has a staged or game quality.

Many others continue the analysis of life as drama. The general perspective influenced a host of Goffman students, such as Arlene Daniels, David Sudnow, John Lofland, Sherri Cavan, Marvin Scott, and Jacqueline Wiseman. Several sociologists, such as Stanford Lyman and Marvin Scott, returned to the theatre in a direct fashion and made explicit use of its imagery in *A Sociology of the Absurb*. And, finally, the inevitable "popularizer" appeared. Eric Berne took the analysis, simplified it considerably, added some cute gimmicks, and sold a million copies. He, however, used the game metaphor, which is indeed similar in that it has the same essential qualities with regard to the individual's relationship to others.

Though Berne's *Games People Play* did serve to spread the metaphor out into the general public, it and the other channels of sociological insights were not the only—nor perhaps the primary—source of the popular idea that life is like a drama. The theatre itself also influenced the masses to compare their lives to the theatre.

HOLLYWOOD

As mentioned earlier, any social segment that is in and around the theatre tends to notice the similarities between theatrical performances and the structure of social life. However, experience with the theatre had generally been restricted to the "leisure classes" until the twentieth century. Then the industrial revolution not only brought new chunks of free time to the lower classes, but produced that marvelous invention, the movie.

When motion pictures appeared, not only had the masses been supplied with more hours away from work, they had been freed from other social involvements and restraints. In particular, the Puritan definitions of the theatre being unserious, time-wasting and evil had lost their force. Then the Great Depression hit and Americans turned to the inexpensive escape which had just reached a new level of sophistication. Consequently, after 1935, movie-going and later watching television became the favorite pastimes of Americans. The influence of Hollywood was on the upswing.[18]

Hollywood and television promoted the theatrical perspective in a more forceful fashion than earlier forms of theatre. Not only did they flood the lives of ordinary people with theatrical renditions of everyday stories with which the masses could identify, but in order to sell the new product on a mass basis, Hollywood developed a "star" system, in which, with the aid of the written media and radio, certain actors and actresses were turned into super-celebrities. For the star system to be a reality, the public had to be inundated with information about the private lives of the stars who, of course, carefully geared those private lives to full publicity potential. Television to a great extent continued this star system. Hollywood, moreover, particularly in the thirties, made as many movies about making movies as any other subject except the Old West. No wonder the lines between the movie and real life became fuzzy in the minds of the stars, who seemed to have extreme difficulty keeping the roles they performed in the movies separate from their other life activities. The publicity about movie-making, the celebrity cults of the stars, and the regular watching of films and TV programs also influenced the movie fans, theatregoers, and television audiences to see "real" life as a theatrical production. Gail Parent has captured this tendency to see life as bits of movies in *Sheila Levine, Is Dead and Living in New York*, a novel about a young lady looking for a husband in New York. Sheila, though she has become cynical about Hollywood's inaccurate characterizations of life, reveals how she used movie sequences as guides to her own life plans:

> My roommate, Linda, and I decided way back in Syracuse that if we weren't married by the time we graduated, we probably could at least be engaged, and we would live together in Manhattan. Why not? Didn't Doris Day always have a precious, little two-bedroom apartment, all yellow and light blue and cuddly? Nothing pretentious—just a modest fifteen-hundred-a-month apartment in a gorgeous brownstone that poor Doris paid for with her unemployment check. The sheets and matching pajamas alone must have cost a fortune. Four years of college apiece, and Sheila Levine and Linda Minsk didn't know that Hollywood had been deceiving them all these years. We thought that if we were good girls and looked hard enough, Doris Day, when she was carried off into blissful matrimony, would sublet her place to us [p. 29].

SELF-CONSCIOUS ACTING

Since the 1950s at least, most ordinary urbanites continually or regularly engage in a style of behavior which has the basic elements of self-conscious stage acting. They perform everyday rituals, deception dramas, and audience-precipitated acts. In many instances, a theatrical mentality has determined the character of their collective solutions to the problems created by structural and cultural dislocations. In order to fill in for the community, the family, and the other "traditional" institutions which formerly supplied them with a network of primary contacts, with collective, expressive activities, with meanings, purposes, a design for living, they have participated in the construction and maintenance of new entities which are more theatrical in nature. These are the scenes which were described fully in the first four chapters. More analysis of these scenes' theatrical characteristics will be presented in the next chapter.

We have shown that dramatists duplicated the structure of interaction in their creation. Now that theatricality is more pervasive and explicit, we should expect a new form of theatre which captures the character of the contemporary style of interaction. As a matter of fact dramatists have not let us down. We have such a theatre and it is valuable in supplying us with new insights into the nature of interaction in the modern city. It is various labelled the new "living theatre," "environmental theatre," or "the theatre of the poor."

THE THEATRE REACHES THE STREETS

In the living theatre, the performers intentionally try to remove the barrier between the audience and themselves, and pull the audience into active participation in the play. The theory is that the drama should not be viewed as a distinctly different enterprise from "real" life, but that the play itself is real. Actors and audience should perform together, in a spontaneous manner, using the structure of the play only as a platform to support their interaction. Moreover, if it seems appropriate and possible, they may break the time and space limitations imposed by the play and the theatre, and carry on the activities they are creating beyond the final curtain. They may even precipitate a significant social event, a demonstration, or a movement. Richard Schechner comments on the interaction between the performers and the audiences in his environmental theatre, a form of living theatre.

> What happens to a performance when the usual agreements between performer and spectator are broken? What happens

when performers and spectators actually make contact? When they talk to each other and touch? Crossing the boundaries between theatre and politics, art and life, performance event and social event, stage and auditorium? Audience participation expands the field of what a performance is, because audience *participation takes place precisely at the point where the performance breaks down and becomes a social event.* [19]

In the theatre of the poor, in which the performers and the audience are often spatially mixed, without the audience being drawn into the performance, there is an attempt to make the actor and the audience more self-conscious of the roles they play in ordinary life. The actors are intensely aware of themselves performing in front of others and, perform ritualistic life sequences in an exaggerated and harsh style. Self-consciousness, according to Jerzy Grotowski, the originator of the theatre of the poor, is a means of acquiring authenticity and freeing oneself from the masks people normally wear in the everyday world.

These two new theatrical developments supply us with insights into emergent forms of everyday acting. On the one hand, consciousness of self as an actor and life as a series of performances allows people who have overcome their fear of the heterogeneous urban world to take advantage of the diversity of urban life. Richard Sennet, in *Two on the Aisle*, has described this new urban condition quite well.

I suspect . . . that cities, when they are open and diverse, can be stages on which people learn to act in the self-conscious way Grotowski practices under very different circumstances. But there is an enormous risk in this dramaturgy. Paris as we know it from the novels of Balzac and Flaubert, Chicago and New York as we know them from Dreiser and Edith Wharton, were cities in which a man or woman could play many different roles, moving, as the sociologist Robert Park put it, from "microcosm to microcosm," from the world of saloons, to union halls, to sporting arenas, for example, appearing as a different character in each setting. But the characters who do not become self-conscious about their role-playing are crushed by the complexity and harshness of city life [p. 31].

On the other hand, self-conscious awareness of the self as an actor and life as a performance allows many people to break the molds, the tightly constructed roles, and, as in the environmental theatre, to create new performances and new scenes. Consequently, *some* of the new scenes in the city are much less tightly written and the actors are freer to engage in somewhat spontaneous acting with others in particular social settings. Certainly, even in the case of the more spontaneous, new urban scenes, there is a general outline of a script and roles, but these are loosely sketched and the most important aspect of some of the new life scenes is creating drama in interaction with other actors.

6 | EVERYDAY ACTING

We have been suggesting for a time now that people increasingly are "on" (that is, performing like actors on stage) in their everyday social interaction. We have already mentioned many aspects and forms of acting, so we must now turn to the task of more carefully identifying the basic characteristics that distinguish acting in everyday life. We must also examine the variations of this social-psychological phenomenon and the different social settings or conditions in which they appear. In closing this chapter and the book we will explore some of the general implications of this new social-psychological behavior mode.

CHARACTERISTICS

The fundamental dimension of acting in ordinary life routines is being conscious of oneself in the presence of others. A second feature, corollary to this fundamental aspect, is that individuals, when on, construct action with the intention of conveying certain impressions about themselves although they may have other aims as well. A third dimension is one we have previously mentioned—that individuals remain aware that they have levels of existence apart from the self they are presenting in a particular setting. We must add one last feature to complete the model. In presenting a self, individuals do not start in each social setting with a clean slate, but occupy a social category with shared meanings, definitions, norms, and roles. These are the basic aspects of acting in everyday life: being self-conscious in the construction of acts, managing self-presentation to the point that one recognizes that one's self is more or less contrived; having a self or selves apart from the immediate action; and being aware of existing social categories.

Many critics of "dramaturgic" sociologists, particularly of Goffman, have argued that the dramaturgists have conveyed a demeaning, derogatory, and narrow conception of human behavior. It's possible to see the outline above as guilty of this same oversimplification. We do not accept these criticisms of the general perspective (even though they do fit much of Goffman's work), but reviewing them can help us develop a fuller understanding of acting in everyday life.

Starting with some of the more general criticisms, Alvin Gouldner has argued in *The Coming Crisis of Western Sociology* that Goffman and the other dramaturgists are caught in the narrow mentality and morality of the new bourgeoisie. He further suggests that in focusing on such a thin slice of life—microcosmic interaction settings—and in characterizing life enterprises as mere drama, Goffman and his like are supporting the status quo of the corporate-dominated welfare state. We take issue with Gouldner's criticism of the dramaturgic theory, but accept his characterizations of the dramaturgists. There is nothing inconsistent with the dramaturgic model and a broader analysis of society or radical social change. It just happens that many of the symbolic interactionists have been interested exclusively in microcosmic phenomena, much of which is trivial. The essential question still remains: Do people interact in a dramaturgic manner?

Another criticism, recently levelled by Richard Sennet, is that Goffman has characterized humans as being caught in a restrictive net of roles and norms, which gives them no freedom for spontaneous, creative, or individual action. We agree somewhat with this criticism as applied to Goffman, but it does not apply to the dramaturgic model in general (nor does Sennet intend it to). It was suggested above that contemporary social phenomena have shifted toward the living theater (which Sennet himself suggests as a comparison to catch contemporary urban sponteneity). Goffman does seem to be caught in a world of small-town bourgeois morality where more restrictive characterization of "place," "role," and "position" figure prominently. In this sense, he can be said to be lagging behind emerging social behavior.

Still another criticism made by John O'Neill, John Helmer, and Richard Sennet, is that Goffman's view of the human being allows no intrinsic human qualities, but only the very ignoble, petty, face-saving, fearful, and unhappy.[3] Goffman certainly has *not* presented a very heroic, endearing, or optimistic view of human beings. By and large, his people are struggling fearfully and desperately to save face, avoid hassles, or make good impressions in spite of their enormous shortcomings. For instance, the physicially deviant person

> gives accounts, belittles his discomfort, and presents an apologetic air, as if to say that in spite of appearance, he is deep in his social soul, someone to be counted on to know his place, someone who appreciates what he ought to be as a normal person, and who is this person in spirit, regardless of what has happened to his flesh [Goffman, p. 351].[1]

The only honorable people in Goffman's work seem to be those like prisoners or mental patients, who accept extreme forms of punishment or psychiatric derogation to preserve their right to be unmanipulated, autonomous beings. Thus, in general, the noblest individual in all of Goffman's work is the one who, in search of freedom, withdraws completely from threatening, insidious, or "phoney" social enterprises. What has been so discomforting to people who read Goffman's books is that most characters are so petty and ignoble, and social life so grim, threatening and shallow. Moreover, Goffman delivers these repulsive characterizations with convincing force and, we suspect, from a fundamentally sound dramaturgic basis. But we do not have to accept his derogatory interpretations of dramatic behavior, because dishonorable or petty forms of acting do not *necessarily* flow from self-conscious acting.

The basic model stated above allows for a wide range of possibilities on each of these issues. For instance, moving in a world where one shifts from social category to social category is not in itself restrictive of freedom. In the first place, the social categories one occupies range from loose, ephemeral, relatively open "identities" to highly specified, closed "roles" in rigid social enterprises. Second, in the modern heterogeneous world, a person has more and more space for bringing individuality to existing social categories no matter how tightly they are structured.

There is a more fundamental point on this issue, however: Freedom and spontaneity are not maximized by the elimination of limits, guidelines, and rules, such as those which social categories introduce into behavioral settings. The absence of limiting dimensions raises the number of conflicting and confusing encounters between individuals to such heights that freedom and spontaneity are impeded.[2] The existence of *some* social guidelines can still leave sufficient space for individual variation, creativity, and spontaneity. In addition, being self-conscious about the nature of the limits and the degree of space increases the potential for individual and spontaneous variation.

Jazz, a highly creative and spontaneous activity, serves as an excellent example of the balance between limits and space in creative and spontaneous action. The best jazz performances occur when a group of highly skilled musicians have demonstrated that no matter what variations each plays, they are all working within a basic melodic, tonal, and rhythmic structure. That structure has been a particular song's chord sequences, the "changes," which each musician keeps in mind and returns to or draws notes from as he travels in and around the melody with his own variations. A certain steady beat has been kept as a reference point and though every instrumentalist adds beats or purposefully plays off beat, each demonstrates clearly to the others that he is keeping track of it. If the changes are not known or referred to regularly, or the beat is lost completely, then the possibilities for mutual trust, creation, and spontaneity are reduced. This relationship can extend to all life situations. Spontaneity occurs within areas set by accepted limits, not in wide open spaces. Lack of limits or disagreement on them will precipitate confusion, fear, suspicion, or embarrassment, which dampen spontaneity. We must not assume, therefore, that performing in a role is necessarily freedom-restricting.

Moreover, behavior engaged in from a more dramatic posture is not necessarily demeaning, shallow, or frivolous. Self-conscious action in social settings can be aimed toward the same variety of ultimate ends as unselfconscious action. I feel Goffman is being too cynical when he writes that face-saving, embarrassment avoidance, place-keeping and the other less admirable and less endearing motives are the ultimate or exclusive purpose of acting in front of others. In reality, people act self-consciously not only to win some petty, self-serving advantage, but also to uphold the most important ideals of their social group, as in the case of ritual performance; to bring about social change, as in the case of radical protest activities; and to be effective in establishing public policies, as in the case of political decision-making.

In addition, the group which is physically present is not necessarily the audience for whom an act is performed; rather the intended audience may be some group not present or some generalized, real, or imaginary group of others—such as "ones colleagues," "mankind," or "future generations." The possibility of acting before these audiences can relegate embarrassment, face-saving, and other selfish pursuits to positions of lesser importance. I think that most admirable individual acts are probably executed with an acute sense of the self in front of audiences and with considerable attention to impression management.

Finally, we argue that the theatrical approach to life is somewhat neutral as it relates to human happiness. We will go into the more general issue of whether modernization and relativization have produced more human despair or more human happiness at the close of this chapter. At this point we will emphasize that both possibilities are open. We should not be depressed that much of human behavior is selfconscious. In the 1950s there was a strong movement to derogate calculated, staged "hypocritical" behavior. The popularity of David Riesman's *The Lonely Crowd* and William Whyte's *The Organization Man*, which exposed "other-directed" people and hollow executives, and of J.D. Salinger's *Catcher in the Rye,* in which Holden Caufield stamped around the society denouncing self-righteous "phonies" was an expression of this collective sentiment. Some of us have learned to accept self-conscious acting, and many are enjoying the possibilities that it has opened up. "Scenes" can be meaningful and satisfying. Tom Wolfe, not Salinger, Riesman, or Whyte, is a better chronicler of the 1960s-1970s, and in his characterizations many people are having a fine time.[3]

DIFFERENT FORMS

RITUAL

The oldest form of drama-like behavior—even predating the actual drama which it spawned—is ritual. Actually, since it is the predecessor and has many of the aspects of real drama, it should not be considered a "everyday" life activity which is merely drama-like. However, in its less-formal appearances, it is indeed acting in everyday life, and we shall include it in our list.

It is clear that ritual has the basic qualities named above. A description of one phase of the elaborate initiation rite of a Melanesian people demonstrates that the individual is self-consciously managing impressions in front of audiences, which in the case of ritual are the gods of the society and the society in general.

> Every villager had to adorn himself, and the canoes too had to be freshly painted with ochre and chalk. Everyone boarded the canoes. The initiate stood in the canoe of his relatives, and the skull was placed before him on the bottom of the canoe. The brothers of the initiate's mother were to stand in front of him; later they would squat. Like an old man, the initiate would lean on a stick on which was set a disk with a hole in the center so that a few inches of the stick would show above the disk. The initiate would hold the stick with two hands somewhere in the middle. Slowly the canoes, manned with drumming and singing villagers, began to move down the river toward the sea—to the west, to where the sun sets.

> The initiate acted like a worn-out old man; he appeared to become weaker and weaker, the farther westward they went. After a while he began to lean on the shoulder of an uncle and finally collapsed and lay down on the bottom of the canoe.

> At that stage he was lifted by one of his mother's brothers and, together with the skull, was immersed for a while in the sea. After he was hauled back into the canoe, all his ornaments were taken off and put in the magic mat; they were never to be removed from it. From this moment on, the skull was no longer used by the initiate; he had to hang it on the breast of a woman, who had asked the owner-hunter for this favor.

> While singing, all turned back toward the land, to the east, to where the sun rises. When they reached the shore, they entered the tide-flooded forest to look for crabs. The initiate joined them, but he had to be careful not to break off the pincers of a crab, as that might cause the death of the headhunter.

> The initiate now acted as a new-born babe, and then as a child who did not know how to handle a paddle. He acted as if he did not know the name of the river and its tributaries, or the names

of the trees. But gradually he seemed to learn more and more. At every tributary his name was called and he answered with his bamboo horn.

Back again in the village he did not enter the bachelors' house, but went to the house of his family. There he was again decorated from head to foot, and now the bamboo plates were hung on his breast while all present sounded a long-drawn "e-e-e-e-e-h." Henceforth the initiate acted as a young man, full of vigor and admired by all.[4]

The purpose of the ritual is a transcendental one—individuals are attempting to move outside themselves, unite with the collectivity, and embrace its meanings, traditions, and mysteries. The script is tightly written. In fact, this is one of the distinguishing features of ritual—the strict re-enactment of behavior sequences.

Ritual ceremony appears in locations other than the society's special, formal arenas. The tendency to ritualize social patterns is a ubiquitous human characteristic. In fact, mundane routines are often elevated to ceremonial levels, and then they become life-drama enactments. Orrin Klapp supplies us with an excellent sample of this process:

The egg cups, pickle caster, and soup tureen figure in a family ceremonial. Mother is the high priestess of this rite. The dinner is served by candle light and the contents of the antique cabinet are emptied onto the table. We eat with the Family Silver off the soup plates my grandparents bought on their wedding day in 1881. We all love this. What is the value of the delightful family mumbo jumbo? It is to a closely knit family like ours what a wedding anniversary is to a couple who love one another very much [p. 123].

DECEPTION DRAMAS

A second, long-standing form of life-drama is the deception drama. In this form of acting, one or more people present a self which is at variance with their usual selves, and they purposefully manage impressions in order to accomplish something which is not openly admissible. Usually (but not necessarily) the goal is some personal gain. Spies pursuing important national goals, for instance, engage in deception dramas (Erving Goffman's newest book, *Frame Analysis,* explores in detail these types of complicated, manipulated "frames."). More often, however, the ends are trivial and self-serving. Eric Berne's popular book is a collection of the typical everyday deception dramas which he calls games. We can pick one as an example:

> First-Degree "Rapo," or "Kiss Off," is popular at social gatherings and consists essentially of mild flirtation. White signals that she is available and gets her pleasure from the man's pursuit. As soon as he has committed himself, the game is over. If she is polite, she may say quite frankly "I appreciate your compliments and thank you very much," and move on to the next conquest [p. 126].

In this example, White is acting as if she is a person interested in establishing a relationship with another person—a man. But she is really interested only in winning satisfaction from the knowledge that she can attract men—an inadmissible purpose. This is a common enough act so that it falls into a class of life-dramas in which most of us engage with some degree of regularity.

The audience in deception dramas is usually the physically present group or some selected members of it. However, deceptions can become very elaborate and be played to a large, dispersed audience, such as in the case of complex con games or espionage.

Some deception dramas involve concerted activity between players. The aforementioned con games and espionage are ideal examples, for their "actors" openly share the actual purposes of their acts with each other and only hide the dramatic nature of their performances and their intentions. These planned collective deception dramas are in a sense real theatrical enterprises.

AUDIENCE-PRECIPITATED ACTS

Another common and ancient form of self-conscious behavior is audience-precipitated acting, which occurs when actors are unusually sensitive to audience evaluation. This form of acting is the most common in everyday life; in fact, it is related to a quality in all interaction—that is, responsiveness to the evaluations of others. In some situations, when the evaluators are particularly judgmental or their judgments are especially consequential to the actor, then the sensitivity to their evaluations is increased and the acting becomes "self-conscious."

Goffman has supplied us with several examples of this type of acting: The mental patient trying to please the therapeutic evaluators in order to be deemed sane, or the physically handicapped person trying to act normal and not be a burden to those around them, so as not to be repulsed and avoided.[5] This form of drama is not always selfish, pitiful, or ignoble. Often it occurs when people believe that their acts have some consequence and, therefore, audiences are watching them with a readiness to judge. For instance, Tom Burns, in a study of the BBC bureaucracy, reports that the executives were self-conscious because of their positions of importance.

> What was apparent in the interviews which form the basis of this study, and what indeed appears in many of the passages quoted, is that people can observe themselves in situations which require them to use their intelligence, skill and knowledge to the full, can feel an 'I' which remains critical and detached from engagements and commitments.

People involved in momentous political events experience similar feelings of self-conscious detachment and carefully manage impressions of self. Hannah Arendt reveals in *On Revolution* that Robespierre was caught in an insoluable dilemma of having to present a virtuous self to the Paris audiences and of being fearful of his own hypocricy:

Since his [Robespierre's] very credo forced him to play the "incorruptible" in public every day and to display his virtue, to open his heart as he understood it, at least once a week, how could he be sure that he was not the one thing he feared most in his life, a hypocrite? [p. 92]

Another variation of this type of acting in everyday life appears in situations in which persons act in front of strangers and are rendered self-conscious because of differences between the definitions imposed on the situation by the strangers and their own taken-for-granted meanings. In my study of released prisoners, I found that in the first few days or weeks after release, persons were estranged from themselves and acted extremely self-consciously.

A final, often more tender example is that of the actor being rendered self-conscious because he or she is trying to convey sincere feelings and thoughts to some other people who are very important. For instance, the young person in love, trying to convince a loved one that he or she is totally sincere, will very often become extremely self-conscious, stilted, or even semi-inarticulate due to his or her *sincerity*, not due to hypocrisy.[6]

The primary goal in this form of everyday drama is not to deceive, or to achieve some inadmissible self-gain, though these may be involved. The primary aim, or an important aim, is to be accepted, esteemed, or at least not ridiculed, rejected, or repulsed by an audience which is actively or potentially judgmental.

NEW FORMS OF ACTING

In the postwar era, with modern media figuring so prominently in people's lives, several new forms of everyday acting have emerged.

Groups that are trying to influence large segments of the

population have discovered that the amounts and type of media coverage they obtain is extremely important to the realization of their goals. Consequently demonstration, strikes, rallies, and news conferences are planned with the intention of drawing TV and newspaper personnel, and making certain impressions for TV and newspaper audiences. The staged activities begin when (not before) the cameras and reporters arrive, and subside when the media personnel withdraw. This relationship between the media and political activities was demonstrated daily at Berkeley and San Francisco during the 1960s, when the student political activities at the University of California and San Francisco State would begin at noon, giving the news people time to arrive and set up, and would wind down shortly before 5:00 p.m. This schedule also gave reporters time to write their stories for the 6:00 p.m. news, when most active participants and spectators ventured to some TV set to see how the events of the day were being shown.

The everyday life-dramas should be viewed as brief interludes or small fragments of life. Activity system scenes, on the other hand, are larger and more complicated dramas. Consequently they possess many more theatrical characteristics.

The activity system is fundamentally theatrical. It involves a self-conscious choice to participate in a scene and a self-conscious management of behavior to perform according to shared meanings and a special language. To some degree, the others participating in the scene, those watching, and all other citizens who are aware of it constitute different types of audiences before whom impressions must be managed. However, we must stress here that, though impression management is an integral part of the scene, the basic mode of interaction is expressive; that is, the participants come together to enjoy the collective activities.

To understand these theatrical aspects of the activity system, it is useful to compare it to the living theatre, a more contemporary form of drama and the form which is most closely related to contemporary urban life. For instance, in considering "scripts" for such activities, it is much more likely that activity system scripts resemble the living theatre than they do the traditional theatre. A script in this case is usually an outline to be filled in by actors during the activities, allowing freedom for a great deal of spontaneous, creative behavior. After an individual acquires some knowledge of the language, meanings, and dress styles, and some skill at an activity, such as skiing, he or she may talk, dress, and behave in a multitude of different ways all of which are contained within the scene's general script. The more knowledgeable have a clearer conception of the script and are freer to innovate within its limits. Some can even attempt to break these and to "rewrite" the script. The situated quality of the activity system relates weakly to all forms of theatre, but the other structural characteristic introduced in the first chapter—the scene's availability—is usefully compared to the living theatre. In the living theatre, anyone can attend, become part of the drama, or even stay on as a member of the company. In the activity system, almost anyone may go to the activities, practice them, learn the meanings surrounding them, and become part of the action.

Many of the categories of people in and around the activity system are like those of the living theatre. First, there are people like directors or producers who have some investment (usually financial) in seeing that the show goes on. In the activity system, these are the owners and managers of activities which involve a business, such as skiing, bowling, drinking, etc. In the case of activities which are not owned (e.g., volleyball at the beach), there are "organizers" who accomplish the minimal tasks which are necessary for the activities (such as bringing the ball and the net). [7] Like their counterparts in the living theatre, the managers, owners, and promoters are more likely to participate in the drama than are those from the traditional theatre. Ski resort owners and managers, for example, are very often avid skiers. In fact, their interest in the activity often precedes their financial involvement.

There is a group of "insiders" in all activity systems who resemble the living theatre's regular actors. Insiders are people who are in and around the activities and the location so much that they are known to the owners, managers, and each other. They join together with the owners and managers in constructing the main action of the scene. Often they occupy key positions, such as those of ski instructors or bartenders. Some become very skilled at the activity and known outside the circle of insiders. They are the scene's stars.

The people who come to the activity system to become part of it but are not known by the insiders or owners are similar to the audiences of the living theatre. In a sense, they remain on the periphery of the central action, and their less-skilled participation often disruptes the play. When it is possible for the insiders to control ingress, they usually try to allow newcomers in only when it is to the insiders' advantage—for instance, when they desire some audience. But when the stage starts getting crowded, insiders usually try to close off the scene. There is usually tension between the insiders and the owners or managers on this issue, because the managers, owners, and promoters have a commercial interest in keeping the scene entirely open and continually expanding.

There is a tendency for larger activity systems to break down into subparts, with little groups of regulars and a large number of fringe participants milling around. This can occur at a single location or across locations when a scene has more than one, as it usually does. Thus insiders become less prominent and more difficult to distinguish. New participants benefit, since it is easier for them to take part in the activities without being subjected to ridicule or exclusion by the insiders. However, it also results in more anxiety over authenticity.

Outside the immediate arena is the world of outsiders, and to a lesser extent the performances are staged for them. This is also one of the intentions (if not the accomplishments) of the living theatre. Many people involved in the living theatre are attempting to carry their productions out into the world and have some impact on the general society. The owners and managers of the activities in the activity systems are trying to reach the general audience for more profits, and the actors, to some extent, are trying to win prestige, respect, envy, or admiration because of their participation in the scene.

In at least one sense, the definition of audiences in activity systems is somewhat more ambiguous from that in the living theatre, because the statuses of company members, the audience, and people outside the theatre are more crisply defined than those of the insider, the fringe participant, and the outsider in the activity system. In the latter case, authenticity is more problematic and negotiable. Consequently, there is more self-consciousness in the performances and all actors to some extent perform.

This scene's structure, like that of the activity system, is basically theatrical in that individuals in the modern urban society recognize "parts" or "roles" contained in lifestyle scenes. If they choose to and if they possess the qualifying attributes—age, money, and class orientation—they may assume one of these roles and perform for short or long periods. As they play out the lifestyle drama, they remain somewhat self-conscious in their parts, and they make key choices; such as where to live, how to decorate their house, what to wear, what job, hobby, or activity system to select, what and where to eat, even what to say. They make these choices according to script of their lifestyle scene.

As mentioned earlier, the script which is disseminated largely by the mass media varies greatly in clarity and cohesiveness. Even in the case of the more cohesive and lucid scenes, scripts leave broad spaces for experimentation and spontaneity. So here also the performances are more like those of actors in the living theatre than in the traditional theatre.

Another reason the living theatre is a better model to represent the performances in lifestyle scenes as well as activity system scenes is that the relationship between actors is often more expressive than instrumental. In other words, in performing in a scene, actors come together and interact more for immediate gratification than the accomplishment of some collective task. There are some instrumental activities, particularly economic, contained in these scenes, but most of the group activities and the scenes' general mode are expressive. In the case of expressive activities, unlike the instrumental, there is no "functional" requirement to divide tasks and fulfill minimum organizational needs. People can just be together—talking, sharing meanings, engaging in other expressive activities—and the scene will continue. Consequently, the "roles" are not like those in traditional drama, which has special integrated parts for each actor (and not like the roles in "social system" analysis which borrows its imagery from ancient theatre). The category for the individual in these scenes is more usefully viewed as a loosely defined "identity" within a configuration of cultural meanings, values, and beliefs which permit people with the same or similar identities to engage in expressive behavior.

The audience to the performance in lifestyle scenes break into three categories similar to those in the activity systems. There are the actors themselves, who are audiences to each others' performances. Other scene performers are an especially important audience in face-to-face performances, because the boundaries of the scenes—its script—are constantly being tested and changed. The next category of the audience is the real or imagined world of other performers in the lifestyle who are spread out geographically and who might become witnesses to an individual's performance. (This audience corresponds to the concept of "reference world" described by Shibutani and mentioned earlier.) At the outer fringes is the larger audience of the general society. One of the purposes of adopting a role in a lifestyle scene is to have an identity to present to all other people, present or not. Performances are therefore geared, to a lesser degree, to the entire society.

DIFFERENCES BETWEEN EVERYDAY DRAMA AND ACTUAL THEATRE

In real drama there is a bracketing of the activities—a definition of the situation agreed upon by the audience and the actors in which all that occurs during the drama, though it is real in a sense, it is not actually real.

> Everything that happens on the stage can be called real, because it can be seen and heard to happen. It is perceived by the senses and is therefore as real as anything that happens outside the theatre. On the other hand there is an agreement between all those who take part in the performance, either as actors or spectators, that the two kinds of real event inside and outside the theatre are not causally connected. Dislocation is ensured both because nobody really believes the actors to be the people they represent and because action that significantly alters the state of the situation, such as murder, death by other causes, copulation and birth, are always simulated. [Elizabeth Burns, *Theatricality*, p. 15].

We may see acts in the everyday world as "put on," "phoney," or "nothing but acts," but we still impute a type of reality to them which makes them more real than acts on the stage. This distinction is not always perfectly crisp, but generally it permits us to differentiate everyday acting from real drama.[8]

A second quality, which follows from the first, is that of *irreversibility*. Acts performed in the everyday world become part of one's biography *forever*, but this is not true on the real stage. The acts there (unless we are speaking of the particularities of the actor's performance) belong to the play, not to the actor.

NEGOTIATIONS

The new, urban social-psychological orientation of being self-conscious in constructing action manifests itself in another general and profound manner—the greatly increased number of negotiations that individuals perform in the course of immediate action or in planning future action. In understanding this phenomenon, it is useful to examine the experiments of Harold Garfinkel in the late 1950s and early 1960s. Garfinkel, recognizing that there is a huge chunk of unexploited social ground upon which visible social structures rest, contrived situations which exposed the taken-for-granted assumptions of the unsuspecting. In one experiment, his students, while in a conversation with an acquaintance, moved closer and closer until their noses were almost touching the acquaintance's. In other experiments, students would refuse to accept the usually unquestioned, taken-for-granted meanings which allow conversations to flow smoothly and efficiently. When greeted with the usual niceties such as "how are you?" the student responded: "How am I in regard to what? My health, my finances, my school work, my peace of mind, my . . . ?"

We can learn two lessons from these and other similar experiments. First, the people being encountered in these unusual ways were initially upset and found that when taken-for-granted underpinnings were persistently ignored, interaction was extremely difficult. But, interestingly—and this is our second lesson—the initially disturbed people were often able to struggle through the encounters by making adjustments in their definitions of the situations. In most of the encounters, there was a persistent effort made to get the interaction back on a smooth track. Garfinkel refers to this as the tendency to "normalize" situations.

What Garfinkel accomplished in these years, which is often the case in social science, was to lead an advancing trend. During the sixties, and on into the seventies, his experiments were duplicated in the everyday world by the regular practice of humorous, aggressive, or violent breaking of established interactional routines and propriety. These processes became more widespread with the full recognition of urban heterogeneity, the increased social and geographical mobility, the spread of subcultural relativism, and the emergence of rage and a sense of injustice among segments which were discovering that their relative position was one of unfair disadvantage, deprivation and oppression. The forms of these breaches of taken-for-granted meanings ranged from "putting people on" or refusing to accept statements as their face value—as in the coffeehouse or cocktail "game" of asking what one *really* means—to demonstrations, sit-ins, and mau-mauing. Moreover, once the taken-for-granted foundations had been delivered some initial destructive blows by social scientists, the hip crowd, and cadres of activists, many of the solid structures of public social life began to disintegrate. As this occurred, more and more people began to rummage around in the damaged edifices of social life, playing havoc with the secure, the unquestioned, the sacred, and the accepted substructures of public order. More precisely, the shared rules of propriety governing most social interaction, the shared values which undergirded this system of "norms," and the shared cognitive systems out of which sense was made of social situations and life in general were regularly, intentionally, and irreverently violated. The result has been that many areas of life which were secure have become problematic. This, in turn, resulted in urban individuals' lives being filled with negotiations through which they attempt to keep their lives running along as smoothly as possible.

To thoroughly understand this new everyday phenomenon of negotiating—which, we are suggesting, is closely akin to acting in social situations—we must examine three different levels of social material which were formerly taken for granted and which are presently being negotiated much more often. The first of these is the top, more obvious and immediate layer of social definitions—the norms. Modern urbanites frequently find themselves confronted, put upon, besieged, insulted, or threatened by people who refuse to follow the definitions of proper behavior, the "shoulds" and "musts" which normally obtained in public and private interaction. For instance, in the early 1960s, middle-class white kids began panhandling people in respectable places, such as the financial district in San Francisco. Upper-middle-class professions picketed banks. Students insulted professors and disrupted classes. Armed black men entered the state capitol building in California and threated the assembly members. Muggers spread their activities out to neighborhoods which had previously been considered safe. In general, there has been a tremendous increase in the instances in which strangers obtrusively or aggressively penetrate the normative membranes which used to separate them and regulate the flow of interactional material between friends and acquaintances.

The responses to these intrusions have been diverse. Most modern urbanites have developed a remarkable capacity to disattend. My wife witnessed an occurrence on a New York IRT subway which demonstrated this ability even in extreme circumstances. Shortly after the peak rush hour, a derelict, who was stretched out on a bench in the train and taking several spaces while the standing crowd ignored him, began to rustle around with his fly. Suddenly, while still lying down, he took out his penis and urinated on the floor of the train. The crowd quickly scurried in both directions away from the man. But *they did not utter one word to each other about this event.* After making the necessary adjustments in their spatial relationships with this repulsive stranger, they returned to full disattention.

In other intrusions, in order to negotiate a new comfortable situation, some interaction with the stranger may be necessary. In the early 1960s before the flood of hippie panhandlers ruined such techniques, in San Francisco's North Beach area, I witnessed a panhandler capitalize on the desire of the stranger to normalize the situation. Dressed with intentional shabbiness, the panhandler approached a well-dressed group about to enter one of the moderately expensive restaurants in the neighborhood, told them how hungry he was, and requested that they take him to dinner with them. In their desire to separate themselves as quickly as possible from a repulsive man with an outlandish proposal, they gave him enough money for a dinner, much more than he would have received if he had just asked for money. The prospect he presented blurred their capacity to see that he was just a panhandler with a gimmick, whom they could brush aside as easily as any bum asking for money.

In other instances, the effects of the intrusion are devastating. Le Jeune and Alex studied muggings which occurred in places considered to be safe by the victims and discovered that the people suffered from lingering feelings of fear and insecurity because they had been threatened or actually harmed in settings in which their safety had been taken for granted (*Urban Life,* October 1973). Knowledge of these types of threatening intrusions spread through a community and a general fear and preparedness grows. It is my and others' observation that New Yorkers when walking alone typically look back over their shoulders when they hear someone approaching them from behind. Now people think San Francisco has a very high rate of random street crime and they are taking similar precautions.

In general, the more frequent public breaches of norms have resulted in a much greater attentiveness to surroundings, and more often people find themselves having to normalize damaged social situations. To do this, they often have to negotiate a new set of rules which will work in the shattered situation. Ad hoc occasions and ad hoc decision-making are becoming more common in the modern urban setting.

Besides meeting challenges to normative systems, urbanites must endure frequent and systematic attacks on their values. The members of bohemian, dropout, activist, and unconventional religious groups, who have proliferated in recent years, have not been quiet about "doing their own thing." Instead, they audaciously flaunt themselves, their practices, and their ideas in front of "squares," or aggressively proselytize new members. Their obtrusiveness presents all citizens with gnawing challenges to their own values. A policeman interviewed by Studs Terkel in the 1960s for *Division Street America* reveals how his son's and other youths' attitudes and activities had called his own values into question:

> I was surprised to see what these young people were thinking. Civil rights. Some couldn't care less. Others were militant. Then others like himself [his son] approved of what was going on but didn't participate. They had some very good ideas about it. Some of the most controversial things. Vietnam, Cuba.
>
> But their level of conversation is much higher than the adults' level today.
>
> Until recently, being a policeman was a wonderful thing.
>
> The younger generation doesn't think too highly of us. [pp. 115 and 109].

During the 1960s, articulate radical spokesmen publically attacked sacred American values of individualism, capitalism, and competition; hippies smoked marijuana in front of large audiences and attacked the hypocritical, puritanical values of middle Americans; and angry blacks and other third worlders accused all whites of systematic and destructive racial prejudice and discrimination. Americans have been told that their "good life," which is a dream fulfilled, has damaged, perhaps irreparably, the very earth we live on, has held millions of people in starvation, or at least threatens to expend the world's limited resources and embark us on an age of starvation, social upheaval, and perhaps ultimate extinction.

There are no sanctuaries left today where people can go on thinking that their values are unchallengeable. In conversations after dinner, at cocktail parties, at local taverns, on subways, and on the sidewalks, the formerly secure, taken-for-granted values of American society are regularly called into question. A convincing proof of the pervasiveness of this is the existence and popularity of programs such as "All in the Family," "Maude," and "Sanford and Son"—in which, on a regular basis, America's sacred cows are brought out and kicked all over the place. Homosexuality, abortion, racial bigotry, Women's Liberation, cheating on taxes, and extramarital sex have all been the topics of these shows. As these are the most popular shows on TV, we can assume that it is impossible to live in our society today and not be forced to regularly renegotiate social values and views of self relative to these values.

Finally, our most profound layer, which contains the taken-for-granted definitions and meanings regarding the physical nature of the world, is continually being disturbed and has to be restructured by us in our ongoing interaction in the urban world. This is particularly disturbing because of the illusion of solidity which this layer presented. It was much more apparent to us that norms and values were shifting and unsafe, but we were certain that what was, *was*. The physical world and its relationships are out there, solid. However, as modern theories of knowledge suggest, individuals perceive the exterior world and its events as solid by means of their own capacity to impose a system of categories and meanings which exist only in the individuals' heads.[9] Things and events are neither neutral nor solid, but instead are vague and ambiguous. They must be filtered through grids of human perspectives before they make any sense at all. Individuals make *mutual* sense out of phenomena only because systems of cognitive categories and meanings are acquired by them in interaction with each other.

Today differentiation, in cognitive systems has developed almost as fast as differentiation in normative and value systems. The proliferation of alternative cosmological and epistemological schemes has been intense in the last two decades. The Judeo-Christian, scientific, pragmatic rationalism which had dominated American and European cognitive systems has experienced serious challenges from many sides. Scholarly proponents of various mystical systems have argued that this scientific-rational cognitive perspective has been a false consciousness which has led man to ignore more important, valid, and human forms of knowledge[10]

At the popular level, a storm of counter cognitive schemes has blown over us. Astrology, Hindu mysticism, religious fundamentalism, and witchcraft have gained millions of devotees. In the 1950s President Eisenhower made the statement that anyone who wasn't a Christian or a Jew should be ashamed of themselves; if he said that today, he would be laughed at by millions.

But this is differentiation at the abstract philosophical level. Does it have anything to do with everyday life? Isn't it true that day-to-day events continue with an extremely high degree of consensus regarding their nature? The answer to this is an emphatic *no.* In the first place, this consensus was to a great extent an illusion generated by general consensus in cognitive categories. In actuality, to every event or sequence of events there have always been as many interpretations as there are observers, and the "truth" has to be negotiated as the events unfold. Formerly, there was more consensus in the systems of meaning and values which guided these sense-making processes. In recent years, however, counter systems have sprung up, and the swift movement to consensual versions of things has been disrupted. [11]

In the everyday world, this means that some individuals have been cut loose from a cognitive web-spinning process which formerly gave them and the world the appearance of static design. This has freed them to explore the possibilities of a multiplicity of ways to see things. They can more easily reject yesterday's consensus, about themselves and the world.

Some advantages of this are obvious—it is much more difficult to impute insanity, or to impose oppressive orthodoxy. Areas of cognitive creativity have been widened. However, individuals have also been set adrift in a sea in which the visibility is poor and the going hazardous. And they cannot simply rely on the collective process for navigating. In actuality, the collective process of exchanging reality systems was always somewhat precarious because it relied so heavily on subtle cues, inuendo, and obscure messages. Thus, many people were left out, confused, or even driven mad. [12] But now, with cognitive pluralism and relativism, the going is even rougher. To a much greater extent, people must *individually* grapple with their perceptions, struggle to keep these straight, and pick among the many interpretations offered by friends, strangers, and "experts." They may embrace or re-embrace new or old ideologies—e.g., Christian fundamentalism—to help them make sense out of the world. However, relativism has a way of persistently undermining commitment to these pat schemes, and often after a series of attempts, people end up trying to negotiate their own truths.

Such is the case as regards all these different layers of social categories—norms, values, and cognitive meanings. Contemporary urbanites, in coping with a confusing modern world, regularly find themselves negotiating and renegotiating, with themselves and others, what is the appropriate behavior in particular situations, what are the important things to cherish and respect, and what is actually going on around and within them.

FREEDOM AND DESPAIR

One last important question remains regarding the new social-psychological orientation. Has the modern urban condition improved individuals' lives by opening up new areas of freedom and variety, or has it plunged them into a profound despair by casting them off secure platforms of meaning and values? This controversy predates the industrial revolution. Two of the important enlightment philosophers—Montesquieu and Rousseau—took opposing views on this issue. In *The Politics of Authenticity,* Marshall Berman brings their contradictory ideas together. Montesquieu, speaking through a Persian king, offers a view of emptiness and oppressiveness of traditional society, in which there is

> a uniform existence, without enjoyment, everything smells of obedience and duty. Even the pleasures are sober, and the joys severe, and they are practically never relished except as manifestations of authority and subservience.

On the contrary, lively, vital, liberated Paris is experienced by the king as a place where the human can find real excitement in living.

Two decades later, Rousseau saw it differently. The city, the masses, the crowds, the superficiality of civil society kept humans from discovering their natural beings. Modernity had replaced traditional identities which were "stagnant and rigid as stone," with

> a form of identity as transient and insubstantial as the wind. Modern man's sense of himself was entirely relative, a function of his momentary success or failure in competition for property and power against his fellowmen [Berman, p. 313].

The industrial revolution, which raised urban poverty, density, squalor and ugliness to new levels, produced a long series of deplorers of modernization. In the nineteenth century, many sympathizers of the old European aristocratic social order bemoaned the emergence of the uncultured bourgeoisie and the complete liberation of the urban masses. This, they argued, created a vulgar and politically unstable condition. Without the rigid, elite-dominated social order, the "third estate" became an aimless, normless, atomized, and ignorant mass which vulgarized life and remained highly susceptible to demagogues who would lead it to overthrow the existing bourgeois leaders and institute excessive totalitarism.

The works of many of the important early sociologists, such as Tönnes, Weber, Durkheim, and Marx, dealt primarily with the new social forms emerging in the industrial and urban revolutions, and directly or indirectly with the theme of alienation of human beings because of modernization. A great part of *American* sociology since its inception in the late nineteenth century has been a thinly disguised lament for the loss of the small, traditional communities and an expression of revulsion for life in large American cities. Some sociologists saw the modern urban condition as one rife with social and personal disorganization, caused by disintegration of the basic social institutions, such as the family, the primary group, the church, and the community. They saw suicide, crime, insanity, dereliction, prostitution, and all the other major "social problems" as outcomes of social and personal disorganization. [13] Many of the early American sociologists, suggested that this disorganization was temporary and new sets of institutions were emerging in the urban setting, and they worked to remedy the urban problems they saw. However, in spite of their more optimistic forecasts, their characterization of the individual's plight in the modern city was one of lament.

More recently, the theme of the individual being separated from a natural, true, or real self has been pursued by psychoanalytically oriented deplorers. Karen Horney and Erich Fromm, for instance, argued that the modern condition jarred the human being off a natural developmental track and produced individuals who are alienated from themselves. Horney, in *The Neurotic Personality of Our Time,* suggested that competition which pervades the modern society has exaggerated the need for acceptance and approval which leads to a "neurotic personality." Fromm argued in *Escape from Freedom* that in the capitalist system of production the human has become an end, separated from his work, and, therefore, objectified and alienated from his true self.

In the last two decades, sociology has produced several rather complex theories of alienation. David Riesman argues that the modern industrial society has produced a human without solid tradition or basic values to guide him. Instead, he has been equipped with a radar-like sensor system which searches for immediate approval in particular situations. This type, Riesman suggests, is better suited to participate in the complex, rapidly changing organizations in the modern world.

Orrin Klapp, in *Collective Search For Identity* offers a more complete theory of alienation and one which has many similarities to the theory of acting presented in this study. He suggests that the modern individual grows up in a world in which all the mechanisms and processes that gave meaning to life and an identity to the individual have been weakened or destroyed. In the first place, the explosion of knowledge has reduced in importance the history of any particular group. Constant and rapid change have destroyed places—such as houses, streets, and towns—which served as concrete and symbolic reference points for significant events and stages in individuals' lives. Moreover, the greatly increased social and physical mobility has translated people into social categories, and the people occupying these categories relate to each other only on very narrow issues. Finally, there has been a disappearance or depreciation of the identifying rituals which served to intensify the individual's "awareness of shared mystiques or awareness of himself as a person" (pp. 33-34). All of this has created severe identity problems for a significant portion of the population, and many of the people experiencing these problems embark on frustrating, at times silly, collective searches for identity.

On the other hand, there are some celebrators of the urban condition. Their analyses avoid the descent into the personality, or the inner self, and on the sunnier surface of life they find greater amounts of freedom, excitement and variety in the postindustrial city. The deplorers attributed the modern individual's problems to the identical conditions that these celebrators applaud: increased social and geographical mobility, privacy, anonymity, and heterogeneity. For instance, Scott Greer, a student of the city, comments on the expanded areas of freedom in modern urban life:

> This freedom is, however, a considerable area of the average person's life space. It is manifest in the metropolitan resident's ability to choose marriage or single status, children or not, large family or small. It is also apparent in his freedom to choose his local residential area, and his degree of participation in its social structure—his lifestyle [p. 104].

Harvey Cox takes issue with the detractors of urban life, about the evils of anonymity and mobility in *The Secular City*:

> How often has one heard that urban man's existence has been depleted and despoiled by the cruel anonymity and ceaseless mobility of the city? How frequently is urban man depicted by his detractors as faceless and depersonalized, rushing to and fro with no time to cultivate deeper relationships or lasting values? Anonymity and mobility can of course become damaging, but since they have been made into anti-urban epithets it is even more important to examine their positive side. Anonymity and mobility contribute to the sustenance of human life in the city [pp. 33-34].

He goes on to denounce small town sociability, which "can mask murderous hostility."

Jane Jacobs pins the superiority of urban life on its diversity in *The Death and Life of Great American Cities,* and defends its privacy and anonymity because they allow individuals to have contacts with a wide variety of people and still maintain control over the flow entering and leaving their lives.

Finally, Tom Wolfe, a leading advocate of the varied, highly mobile, anonymous condition, condemns in *Pump House Gang* the "communitas" and describes one of the delights of the heterogeneous urban world—the proliferation of new lifestyles.

The community has never been one great happy family for all men. In fact, I would say that the opposite has been true. Community status systems have been games with few winners and many who feel like losers. What an intriguing thought—for a man to take his new riches and free time and his machines and *split* from *communities* and start his own league [p. 3].

This controversy between the supporters and detractors of modern urban life begs for solution, but there is none. As in the case with all life dilemmas, both sides are credible. The city is a location of greater privacy, heterogeneity, freedom, and anonymity, and it can indeed be enjoyed. However, the expense of these qualities is that individuals are more likely confused, alienated, lonely, and desperate. This is part of the tension of the city, the price we pay. Along with negotiating, self-conscious acting, and scenes, confusion and loneliness are essential features of contemporary urban life.

Conclusion

At present, the deplorers of the city *seem* to be routing the celebrators. In achieving this apparent advantage, they are armed with the evidence of two recent trends in America: the flight from the cities, and the return to religion. Both are interpreted by many as indicators that people are generally disillusioned with urban life and are longing for the small community. They conclude, therefore, that the city has failed.

As a supporter of urban life, I disagree with the conclusion that these trends indicate people were better off in the pre-urban condition, immersed in a small, homogeneous community with a stable and mystical belief system, or that there will be an enduring movement away from cities. The apparent flight from the cities need not be interpreted as a flight from urban life. Urbanization has freed itself from the city—at least from the inner city. With modern means of transportation and communication, the urban process, which rests largely on rapid exchange and information flow among a large, diverse, and specialized population, has extended itself to the suburbs, the surrounding towns, even into the hinterlands. I think the new patterns of movement from the city mean that now many affluent Americans have discovered they can have it both ways—they are not returning to true rural life; they are just moving to the suburbs, where they can avoid the current severe "problems" of the city (e.g., crime and pollution), have some of the advantages of the smaller community, and still be in quick reach of the downtown theatres, restaurants, and stores.[1] Add to this capability the shopping malls—which bring most of the city's commodities and many of its activities to the suburbs—television, radio, phones, and newspapers, and it's evident that the people who

225

seem to be fleeing the city have really not left at all. While the city is losing population, it retains its intellectual and artistic centers. Moreover, there is now a counterflow, admittedly not as large as the flow outward, back into the city on the part of young adults who are moving into the new high rises and townhouses, and seeking the more intense action of the city.

With regard to the other trend—the massive return to religion—I shall posit the ancient analogy of the pendulum. In the early 1960s, the pendelum swung far and fast toward relativism, secularism, liberalism, and radicalism. Many newly liberated people rushed out to plan and execute the dismantling of the political and social structures which, from their new perspective, seemed so obviously irrational and unjust. However, they were not adequately prepared for a life without the old limits on individual expression, and they had no workable plan to replace the existing political and social institutions. In the first several years of near Dionysian debauchery or extreme political activism, love turned to hate, youth to derelection, unity to factionalism, and civil disobedience to terrorism. In disgust, the "liberated," and many of their peers and elders, watching from the sidelines, recoiled, and turned back to the safety of old-time religion.

Actual and analogous pendulums never swing all the way back. Keep in mind that a very large segment, perhaps half, of the population have *not* turned to pentacostal religion (some percentage still holds to the older, conventional forms). More important is the fact that the inexolerable forces of urbanization (or its nobler synonym, civilization) are in the opposite direction from mysticism and dogmatism. After some period of reaction, the movement back may lose its momentum and then the swing may start forward again. Those who have not lost their commitment to urban life may be joined by growing numbers of people who have become weary of chasing old-time religion, and together they can continue the search for a human posture which is appropriate for living in the modern world. It is certain that it will not be imitative of old models, such as the "born again Christian" or the member of rural community.

This new public stance may well grow at least partially out of the type of acting we have examined in the last chapter. Urban people will increasingly make decisions, select courses of action, choose careers, and generally act with a definite sense of performing in front of others and with a concern for these others' evaluations. Urban life promotes and requires this, and there is no turning back from the city without turning far back. The audiences will get bigger—in fact, may eventually include all humankind. A growing appreciation of other people, promoted by more mobility, education, and knowledge and of global interdependence promoted by continuing worldwide crises like the energy crisis will bring this about. This will result in a very different bond between members of a society. In the past people were held together and made the sacrifices group living required largely because they were close to each other, had a sense of community, and to a degree shared a group consciousness. Later when societies grew and became more complex people were held together by the power of their government, and other social institutions, such as the church and schools. The power of these did not rest solely on the exercise or threat of coercive force. Citizens believed in their institutions, leaders, and national purposes. We have described how these bonds have been weakened or severed.

The new urban masses will reconnect with others on a large scale in a much more voluntary manner when they develop a fuller understanding of the necessity to do so and when they appreciate and tolerate other people more. Instead of withdrawing to smaller circles, such as the privacy of their families and homes, they will enter larger and larger arenas prepared to act self-consciously and humanely.[2] One will have to be the political arena. People have learned that they cannot trust their leaders. Now they must learn that the only remedy for this is to stay active and constantly watch those leaders.

The expressive, leisure activities I focused on in this book are useful preparations for this new type of community based on self-conscious acting. What is going on at present is that the new masses, the middle and working classes, for the first time are learning to live in the cities and enjoy the amenities it offers as well as endure the problems it has created. They are learning to cope with heterogeneity and impersonality, and to develop new modes of collective expression. These scenes are transitional forms of public life. More serious activities will evolve from them, though, hopefully their expressive side will not disappear. At present they may seem contrived, crude, and excessively commercial, but they are teaching people how to "act" in a complex, dense, heterogeneous urban world.

Notes

NOTES TO CHAPTER 1

1. Most of the sociological studies of the city treat it primarily as an instrumentality or "functional" entity. See, for instance, Lewis Mumford *The City in History* (New York: Harcourt Brace, 1961); Gideon Sjoberg, *The Pre-industrial City* (New York: The Free Press, 1965); and Scott Greer *The Emerging City,* (New York: The Free Press, 1965) for leading examples.

2. These and other dimensions of the scene will be examined more thoroughly in Chapter 2, after we have supplied some descriptions of actual scenes to prepare for this later discussion.

3. As we proceed we must bear in mind that everything I describe may end suddenly or grind slowly to a stop. Citizens of the modern, affluent states—particularly Americans—may soon witness the collapse of their economic dream worlds, or some new national purpose may sweep them away from the expressive, leisure activities. This already may have begun with the "energy crisis," inflation, and the apparent decline in the general standard of living. However, it has not yet ended, and we still live in an age of leisure.

4. This discussion of risk was drawn heavily from Erving Goffman. See "Where the Action is," in *Interaction Ritual* (New York: Doubleday, 1967).

5. This discussion borrows heavily from Erving Goffman's more thorough analysis of this phenomenon in *Relations in Public* (New York: Harper and Row, 1971). See especially p. 207.

NOTES TO CHAPTER 2

1. These conclusions regarding patterns of participation were based on summaries presented by Scott Greer, *The Emerging City,* pp. 90-92; and Claude Fischer, *The Urban Experience,* pp. 133-49.

2. Many people (particularly sociologists) will want to know precisely where the scene as the term is used here fits into the complex (and often confusing) bank of sociological concepts. Both manifestations of a scene—the activity system and the lifestyle—involve a configuration of values, beliefs, symbols, meanings, or patterns, and in this way make up a subculture. However, these are *special* subcultures in that they have been identified and at least partially understood by large numbers of people in and around them. Visibility is a fundamental condition of the concept. In this regard, they are much like the *social worlds* presented by Shibutani in his article on "reference worlds" referred to earlier.

In addition, scenes exist in a social context in which there are many social worlds known to many actors. Moreover, they are viewed as being at least somewhat available. This also is fundamental to the concept. As indicated in the preceding chapter, the degree of openness of activity systems may be variable, but all such systems are at least somewhat available to large segments of the population. This makes them *scenes.*

A related characteristic to visibility and openness is that of alterability. Many urban actors feel free to pick and choose among the various scenes, to try several out, simultaneously or sequentially, and to follow one while knowing that they may change scenes eventually. This is definitely an altered social posture and one which will be analyzed more completely in the final chapter.

Activity systems and lifestyle scenes differ in that one is confined to a set of meanings, patterns, and other dimensions which surround one or a few activities, almost invariably expressive, leisure activities; and the other involves a complete or near complete life. The activity system is perceived as a subpart of life's total range of activities. The lifestyle is recognized to include not only a configuration of patterns, values and beliefs, but also a full life design, a world view, and an identity for the individual.

Both scenes are used primarily as expressive vehicles—that is, they are not used as a means to other ends, but as pleasureful ends in themselves. This is particularly true of the activity system, but it is also true to a great extent of the lifestyle. The lifestyle does involve an occupation or at least a means of support, but even here there is considerable emphasis on the "meaningfullness," the "excitement," or the "enjoyment" of the work. Moreover, much more emphasis is placed on the nonworking aspects of the lifestyle: the home and its aesthetic and entertainment values, and the leisure, entertainment activities. As evidence of this emphasis, look at the section most city newspapers carry and call either "lifestyle" or "scene." It invariably deals with fashions, cooking, home decoration, travel, entertainment, and other expressive activities.

3. It must be emphasized that their variety and accuracy are not as great as in the motion pictures. On television, exaggerated and distorted versions of bland, conformist, or excessively consumer-oriented lifestyles have dominated both commercials and programming.

4. Many studies spanning several decades have demonstrated this. A.B. Hollingshead, in an early study of the high school called *Elmtown's Youth* (New York: Wiley, 1945) discovered that popularity was the prime value in high school. James Coleman later reaffirmed this finding in *The Adolescent Society* (New York: Free Press, 1962). Hermann Schwendiger, in his study of the Los Angeles adolescent community located a high school system based on popularity, *The Insiders and The Outsiders: An Instrumental Theory of Delinquency* (unpublished doctoral dissertation. Los Angeles: UCLA 1963).

5. Several movies have presented good descriptions of the high school social world. "Rebel Without a Cause" in the 1950s and more recently "American Graffiti" were excellent in capturing what I see as invidious sociability patterns. However, none to my knowledge has successfully revealed the essentially class-related dichotomy of the high school scene.

6. In a study of emerging patterns of the 1970s, Daniel Yakelovich confirms that most of these shifts are occurring among the general college student population.

7. Yankelovich discovered that college youth in the 1970s had an increased

appreciation of the "ability to express" oneself (ibid.) and that "love and friendship" remain important social values among them (p. 58).

8. Reported by Jim Schermerhorn, "Drug Center Got Fort in Trouble," *San Francisco Examiner and Chronicle* (April 16, 1967) p. 2, sec. 1.

9. In a study of California felons, I discovered a category of "Disorganized Criminals" who fit this description. They were the largest single category in the prison. See John Irwin, *The Felon* (Englewood Cliffs, N.J.: Prentice-Hall, 1970), pp. 23-26.

NOTES TO CHAPTER 3

1. L. S. Penrose, *On The Objective Study of Crowd Behavior* (London: H.K. Lewis and Co., 1952), as quoted in Ralph Turner and Lewis Killian, *Collective Behavior* (Englewood Cliffs, N.J.: Prentice-Hall, 1957), p. 209.

2. This characterization of the surfing clubs was supplied to me by Leroy Granis and "Hoppy" Schwartz who had been members of the Palos Verdes Surfing Club in the 1930s.

3. As Tom Wolfe commented in his description of Ken Kesey's activities at the formation stages of the hippie scene, it is difficult to believe that the doctors attempted to understand the drugs without ever trying them (*Electric Kool-Aid Acid Test,* p. 38).

4. The importance of territories was stressed by Stanford Lyman and Marvin Scott. ("Territoriality: A Neglected Sociological Dimension," *Social Problems,* 1967).

5. This characterization of Kesey borrows heavily from Tom Wolfe's description (*Electric Kool-Aid Acid Test).*

NOTES TO CHAPTER 4

1. The January 1955 issue of *Skin Diver* had a photo of a surfer with a short caption beneath. The February 1955 issue had several more photos and a short story on surfing.

2. Until the late 1960s and the shift to smaller surfboards, surfers paddled their boards on their knees, which gave them large "surfing bumps" just below the knee and on the foot. These pads of cartilage were one distinguishing mark of a surfer and their size tended to reveal the length of time a person had been surfing.

3. As a matter of fact, it was this early journalistic interest which popularized the name "hippie." Many new bohemians, in trying to describe their lifestyle, referred to their patterns, attitudes, and traits as "hip" to distinguish them from "square" or "straight." Their excessive use of the adjective led the reporters to widely refer to them as "hippies."

4. Presently it may be true that scene consciousness on the part of the media drastically interferes with a scene's growth process, perhaps to the extent that another scene like the surfing or hippie scenes is no longer possible.

5. The loose board is the major source of danger in surfing.

6. As evidence of this shift, the Haight-Ashbury Free Medical Clinic experienced a drastic change from psychedelic drug problems to those associated with speed and heroin after 1969. See "The Haight-Ashbury Free Medical Clinic" in David E. Smith and George R. Gay (eds.) *It's So Good, Don't even try it Once*

232

(Englewood Cliffs, New Jersey: Prentice-Hall, Inc., 1972).

7. San Francisco police statistics indicate that the homicide rate in Haight-Ashbury rose 53% from 1967 to 1968. The rise for the city as a whole was 21% (San Francisco Police Department Annual Reports).

8. It was this polarization that generated the tension, hostility, and intense reaction in George McGovern's 1972 presidential bid. McGovern catered (particularly in the early stages of his campaign) to the hip segment; Nixon, to the straight.

9. I think not, but the possibility exists. And if another Grand scene begins to arise, I know that I personally want to be a part of it.

NOTES TO CHAPTER 5

1. Sebastian de Grazia, *Of Time, Work and Leisure* (New York: Anchor Books, 1964), p. 419. However, the increased "free hours," which have been distinctly separated from work, have been contaminated by the new work ethic. Now there is a tendency for modern workers to keep busy, and to be conscious of and make use of time while not working. This is one of the major themes of de Grazia's study.

2. This characterization of the hardships of "olden times," is, of course, a gross oversimplification. What has been done is to collapse earlier periods of human history and treat their different problems of survival as if they occurred all throughout history. In actuality, there were many long periods of relative economic, political and climatic stability. The middle feudal period in Europe, for instance, seems to have been one of these. However, the point still stands. For the past fifty years in the United States and many of the countries of Europe, the problems of survival have been reduced to one—earning money. And in the United States, at least, except for the 1930s Depression, this has not been relatively difficult for most people to accomplish.

3. The study of sociology was to a great extent created by urbanization and, of course, urbanization has been one of its major foci. The number of studies on this subject, consequently, are virtually endless. Lewis Mumford's *Culture of Cities* and Scott Greer's, *The Emerging City* are books which fill in this very incomplete sketch of urbanization.

4. Studies of actual bureaucratic operations have disclosed that many of the individuals occupying bureaucratic positions have goals other than the stated goals of the organization, display irrational behavior, and form informal subgroups within the organization. All of these "nonrational" or individual-oriented activities, in fact, have a great deal to do with the operation of the organization. We must consider these activities as the persistent aspects of social reality that planned organizational efforts cannot remove. What is important about the rise of bureaucracy is that this system of organization has developed so extensively and had such far-reaching effects on our lives. Our work-world and other compartments of our lives have become extremely specialized and depersonalized because of this organizational style, and we have been influenced to define ourselves as something separate from what we do and the roles we occupy. The list of studies of the informal facet of bureaucracies is long. They include: Rinehard Bendix "Bureaucracy: The Problem and Its Setting," *American Sociological Review* (October 1947), and Philip Selznik, "Foundations of the Theory of Organizations," *American Sociological Review* (February 1948) for a summary of ideas

on formal and informal characteristics of bureaucracies. Also, for one of the best case studies of the informal characteristics of a formal organization, see Melville Dalton, *Men Who Manage* (New York: John Wiley, 1959).

5. For example, in 1974, an intense struggle to keep "subversive" moral and political material out of high schools was being fought by West Virginia citizens. The *San Francisco Sunday Examiner and Chronicle* summarized the events of the week:

> After seven weeks of turmoil and violence here by aroused fundamentalist parents against the introduction of assertedly "dirty," "Godless" and "communist" textbooks in the public schools, the prose and verse to which the antitextbook militants object began to emerge in detail during a series of emergency citizens' committee hearings convened to review the offending passages [Ben Franklin, "The Bitter Battle of the Textbooks," *This World*, Sunday, November 3, 1974, p. 14].

Coincidently, Eldridge Cleaver's *Soul on Ice* was one of the books objected to by the West Virginia citizens.

6. Many dissenters to this view have charged that college, like high school, has had the primary purpose of supporting society's official belief and value systems. It is certainly true that particular college professors and particular conceptual systems taught in college have been supportive of the status quo. It is also true that the earlier explicit purpose of the college was "moral" education. In addition, at present there are other values operating in American colleges, such as the value of scholarly, scientific, and technological education or the values of the various student cultures (including political activism) which vie for dominance. (See Joseph Ben-David, *Trends in American Higher Education,* Chicago: University of Chicago Press, 1972, for a more complete discussion of the values in American college education.) But these are merely exceptions or temporary delays to the overall thrust of the liberal college education. These should be seen as small eddies or pools in the educational currents. The long-term, overall, inexorable flow has been in the direction of an increasingly critical, relativistic viewpoint toward society.

7. For instance, many militarily and economically subjugated "primitive" societies have experienced "millenarian" movements in which they develop a new religion that incorporates some of their old mystical beliefs, borrows aspects of the imperialist society's culture, and foretells of their rise out of subjugation and entry into a wonderful new age. Of course, the messiah cults of ancient Israel were examples of these movements. More recently, the "ghost dance" and other movements among the American Indians, and the cargo cults of Melanesia are instances of millenarian movements through which these societies attempted to recapture or maintain cultural and political autonomy and integrity. There are numerous studies of millenarian movements among colonized people. For an excellent analysis of the cargo-cults of Melanesia and millenarian movements in general, see *The Trumpet Shall Sound* (New York: Schocken, 1968).

8. These ideas on the gypsy boundary maintenance were taken from lectures by David Matza at the University of California, Berkeley, Spring, 1963.

9. S. N. Eisenstadt, in a discussion of moderization of European nations, argues that demystification occurred when the "masses" gained more access to the societal centers—the political, religious, economic, and other institutional

centers—which were formerly only accessible to the elites. This increased access was a result of the democratization of European societies. In the United States, which has been more democratic and less rigidly stratified from the outset, demystification is more a result of the discovery of the diversity within the nation and the world. However, Eisenstadt's general discussion of modernization is excellent and much more thorough than our short treatment. See *Tradition, Change, and Modernity,* (New York: John Wiley, 1973).

10. The presence or absence of an unifying national purpose along with the level of general prosperity are more variable conditions and, therefore, the more immediate "causes" of the outburst of leisure, expressive scene-like entities. The other processes related to modernization and relativization have been working over a longer time span and are not so variable. They are the background "causes" which are producing a growing segment of uncommitted or potentially uncommitted people.

11. Francis Bacon, *The Advancement of Learning,* book II, IV, 2. Thomas Heywood, from the poem "The Author to his Books," *Apology for Actors.*

12. There were historical periods when the theatre was available to the lower classes. The medieval religious plays, for example, were performed for everyone. But those were repetitious, rigidly constructed and were performed usually no more than once a year in particular places. Thus, they did not tend to promote the life-drama comparison. In the liberal Elizabethan period in England, many public theaters, such as The Theater and The Globe, co-existed with the more exclusive private theaters. The public theaters had a seating capacity of up to 3,000 and were open to all classes. However, this period was short and even then drama did not reach anything close to a majority of the population. Even in London, the theatre-going crowd was small. Oscar Brocett wrote: "To hold the interest of the relatively small theatre going public, the companies changed bills daily and added new plays regularly" (*History of the Theatre;* Boston: Allyn & Bacon, 1968). The liberal Elizabethan period was followed by suppression of the theatre as well as other "sinful" and "unserious" enterprises. The Puritans not only suppressed the theatre in England, but they succeeded in stifling its development in the early decades in America. For all intents and purposes, in spite of the few exceptions, the form of theatre which would promote the theatrical insight into the nature of human interaction was not promiment or pervasive among the lower classes until the twentieth century and the appearance of the motion picture.

13. Elizabeth Burns, in her work on the theatrical metaphor (*Theatricality*), notes that this shift in the drama from the religious to the secular in the seventeenth century made the similarity between life and the drama even more apparent, p. 11.

14. Herbert Blumer, a student of George Herbert Mead and the informal leader of the "symbolic interactionists," first supplied this label to this tradition in sociology. It has now become its more or less official label.

15. See Max Weber, *The Theory of Social and Economic Organizations* (New York: Free Press, 1964), Chapter 1, "The Fundamental Concepts of Sociology" for the fullest explication of this concept and of Weber's social psychology. George Simmel, "How Is Society Possible?" *A Collection of Essays with Translations and a Bibliography,* ed. by Kurt H. Wolff (Columbus, Ohio: Ohio State University Press, 1959) pp. 337-356.

16. Symbolic interaction, the sociological perspective which developed at the University of Chicago is broader than the dramaturgic approach. Many other "symbolic interactionists" such as Herbert Blumer, Everett Hughes, Anselm Strauss, Arnold Rose, Tamotsu Shibutani, Gregory Stone, and Ralph Turner have extended the analysis of George Herbert Mead without making explicit use of the theatrical imagery of being primarily concerned with impression management and other more self-conscious aspects of acting. See Arnold Rose, *Human Behavior and Social Processes* (Boston: Houghton Mifflin Co., 1962) for a broad collection of symbolic interactionists' writings.

17. An argument that all social interaction is fundamentally "dramatic" is also made by Robert S. Perinbanayagum in a paper which has been extremely helpful to me in writing this chapter ("The Definition of the Situation," unpublished manuscript, 52 pp.).

18. Gallup Polls have traced the rise of the film and then television to the top of the list of popular pastimes. In 1938, movies were second to reading; by 1974, watching television was first and movies, third. See *the New York Times* (Thursday, March 7, 1974) p. 26.

19. Schechner, *Environmental Theater,* p. 40. This is the theory behind living theatre, though this is not usually what happens. In fact, there is some evidence that many performers in the living theatre themselves become uncomfortable with audience participation. Schechner reports that, in a performance of *Dinoysus,* the "performers began to resent participation, especially when it broke the rhythms of what had been carefully rehearsed" (ibid., p. 44).

NOTES TO CHAPTER 6

1. In another similarly ignoble characterization, Goffman states: "I have argued that the individual does not embrace the situated role that he finds available to him while holding all his other selves in abeyance. I have argued that a situated activity system provides an arena for conduct and that in this arena the individual constantly twists, turns, and squirms, even while allowing himself to be carried along by the controlling definition of the situation. The image that emerges of the individual is that of a juggler and synthesizer, an accommodator and appeaser, who fulfills one function while he is apparently engaged in another; he stands guard at the door of the tent but lets all his friends and relatives crawl in under the flap. This seems to be the case even in one of our most sacred occupation shows—surgery" (*Encounters*, p. 139).

2. Alfred Schutz in an article on the stranger ("The Stranger: An Essay in Social Psychology," *American Journal of Sociology* (May 1944) describes how behavior flow is upset when the stranger does not know the taken-for-granted dimensions which make smooth interaction possible.

3. Tom Wolfe's series of explorations of "scenes," though they catch the staged and sometimes insidious quality of modern life, still present a picture of persons "enjoying" their newly won freedoms. See *The Kandy-Kolored Tangerine-Flake Streamline Baby* (New York: Farrar, Straus & Giroux, 1965); *The Electric Kool-Aid Acid Test* (New York: Farrar, Straus & Giroux, 1968); and *The Pump House Gang.*

4. Rev. Gerard A. Zegwaard, "Headhunting Practices of the Asmat of Neth-

erlands New Guinea" in Andrew D. Vayday, *Peoples and Cultures of the Pacific* (Garden City, N.Y. The Natural History Press, 1968) pp. 427-428.

5. Goffman, however, skips to "ordinary" social settings and focuses almost exclusively on audience sensitivity. In doing so he magnifies audience sensitivity in an attempt to convince us that it is the dominant concern even in these relatively unself-conscious occasions.

6. This type of audience-precipitated acting was suggested to me by David Greenberg.

7. Even in these unowned activity systems, there are "promoters" who have financial interests in the scene. For instance, businessmen manufacture and distribute the nets and balls, and try to influence the volley ball scene, though they cannot control it.

8. When "The Deputy" was performed on Broadway, audiences at times forgot this general agreement, screamed at the actors, and nearly stormed the stage. Curtain calls were taken in street clothes so that the audience could not tell who had played what part. Rhoda Blecker described these responses to me.

9. This particular brand of epistemology has many important proponents. Alfred Schutz is one of the principal ones. See Alfred Schutz, *Collected Papers*, Vol. 1 & 2 (The Hague: Martinus Nijhoff, 1962). For another very clear statement of it, see Peter Winch, *The Idea of a Social Science* (London: Routledge & Kegan Paul, 1958).

10. This is an argument presented by Theodore Roszak in his analysis of the rise of the "counter culture" of the 1960's.

11. Evidence of this is the widely circulated contradictory accounts of some of our major events, such as the John Kennedy, Malcolm X, Bobby Kennedy, and Martin Luther King assassinations. These are merely the tip of the iceberg. All official accounts are now suspect. The Watergate scandal is as much a factor of the mistrust of official accounts as anything else.

12. Edwin Lemert, in a study of institutionalized paranoids, found that many had been excluded by their peers from the subtle feedback systems which ordinarily keep people collectively sense-making. This aggravated the paranoids' difficulties in making sense out of things and propelled them into full insanity.

13. See David Matza, *Becoming Deviant*, for an excellent discussion of this anti-urban bias on the "social problems" of the city of the early sociologists. See also C. W. Mills, "The Professional Ideology of Social Pathologists," *American Journal of Sociology* (September 1943) pp. 165-180.

NOTES TO CONCLUSION

1. The preferred living arrangement for Americans appears to be in the suburbs or a small town *near* a large city.

2. Richard Sennet, in *The Fall of Public Man*, has recently argued that the vigorous public life of earlier eras has given way to private life. Americans, he suggests are withdrawing into narrow little niches of their home and family. He fails to stress that it was a small segment of the society which used to carry on the vital public life and that the new masses are experiencing city life for the first time. The scenes described in this book are bridges to a new vigorous public life.